Post-patriarchal, Post-heteronormative, and Postcolonial Psychoanalysis

Post-patriarchal, Post-heteronormative, and Postcolonial Psychoanalysis considers contemporary efforts to create a post-patriarchal, post-heteronormative, and postcolonial psychoanalytic approach to human suffering.

Débora Tajer examines contemporary psychoanalysis and its future by integrating three key strands of Argentinean cultural discourse: the popularity of psychoanalysis, the active feminist movement, and the burgeoning field of feminist psychoanalysis. Tajer delves into themes of subjectivity, power, gender, and family, revealing the patriarchal, heteronormative, and colonial underpinnings of classical psychoanalytical approaches. She also explores the contributions of theoretical-clinical instruments from a gender and psychoanalytical perspective. Throughout the book, Tajer highlights changes in femininities and masculinities, new family and relationship configurations, current forms of labour insertion, evolving ideals, and new modes of gender identity assumption and sexual expression.

Post-patriarchal, Post-heteronormative, and Postcolonial Psychoanalysis will be of great interest to psychoanalysts in practice and in training. It will also appeal to readers looking to understand Argentinian perspectives on the future of psychoanalysis.

Débora Tajer is a psychoanalyst based in Buenos Aires, Argentina. She is Professor of Public Health and Gender Studies at the University of Buenos Aires.

Post-patriarchal, Post-heteronormative, and Postcolonial Psychoanalysis

Psychoanalysis for All

Débora Tajer
Translated by Jane Brodie

Routledge
Taylor & Francis Group

LONDON AND NEW YORK

Designed cover image: Getty | topform84

First published in English 2025
by Routledge
4 Park Square, Milton Park, Abingdon, Oxon OX14 4RN

and by Routledge
605 Third Avenue, New York, NY 10158

Routledge is an imprint of the Taylor & Francis Group, an informa business

Published in Spanish by Topía as Psicoanálisis para todxs: Por una clínica
pospatriarcal, posheteronormativa y poscolonial, November 2020

British Library Cataloguing-in-Publication Data
A catalogue record for this book is available from the British Library

ISBN: 9781032532783 (hbk)
ISBN: 9781032532790 (pbk)
ISBN: 9781003411253 (ebk)

DOI: 10.4324/9781003411253

Typeset in Times New Roman
by codeMantra

This work has been published within the framework of the Sur Translation Support Programme of the Ministry of Foreign Affairs, International Trade and Worship of the Argentine Republic.

Obra editada en el marco del Programa Sur de Apoyo a las Traducciones del Ministerio de Relaciones Exteriores, Comercio Internacional y Culto de la República Argentina.

To Claudio Erbin, my partner, and Sofia Erbin Tajer, my daughter for the love and companionship.

In memory of Ana Zaltsman, my mother, and Sonia Dragif, my great aunt, who taught me how to play my game, even if I didn't get the best chips in the game.

In memory of Fernando (Fajwel) Tajer, my father, who taught me how to play my game and to allow myself to play when I have the winning chips.
To my friends, who are the best of love.

"I wholeheartedly endorse this book. Necessary because psychoanalysis must reconsider whether the categories it has used to understand gender and sexuality still account for the subjectivities of our century, *Psychoanalysis for All* is a vital contribution. Many conceptual tools that could have been revolutionary have become conservative and normative. Not to mention the fact that psychoanalysis has carried a normative bias since its inception. That's why Débora Tajer proposes a psychoanalysis that is both post-patriarchal, post-heteronormative, and post-colonial. Affiliated with a powerful and creative Argentine tradition of articulating psychoanalysis and feminism, Professor Tajer offers new theoretical and clinical elements for a psychoanalysis that addresses the challenges and difficulties of our time."

Jorge Reitter, *Author of* Heteronormativity and Psychoanalysis: Oedipus Gay

"*Psychoanalysis for All* is a courageous book. Debora Tajer criticizes conservative aspects of psychoanalysis based on colonial, patriarchal and heteronormative bases, without, however, renouncing her passion for this theoretical-clinical work and its transformative power. The experience of a psychoanalytic practice with a gender perspective allows us to face changes in bonds, ideals, identities, sexual practices, work and politics. It is a book that invites young analysts to continue to believe in transformation through words and for experienced analysts to remember to always live up to the subjectivity of their time."

Patricia Porchat, *Psychoanalyst and Professor at the State University of Sao Paulo*

"This original and timely book lucidly demonstrates how psychoanalysis, as well as contributing to colonial and patriarchal gendered oppression, is vital to undoing the psychic damage this does. Through meticulous clinical and conceptual analysis, Debora Tajer persuasively shows what postcolonial, feminist and trans-supportive psychoanalytic practice looks like, as grounded in and engaging with local material-political conditions and practices. This vital contribution revises what therapeutic work should and can be. It should be read by all who counsellors and psychotherapists."

Erica Burman, *Group Analyst and Professor of Education, University of Manchester*

"Debora Tajer's book brings to an English-speaking readership important contributions to psychoanalysis of the Argentine School of Psychoanalysis and Gender. She explores the marks of patriarchy, heteronormativity, and coloniality within traditional psychoanalytic theory and clinical process and develops a gender-conscious psychoanalytic interpretation of contemporary gender roles, sexualities, and family forms. Tajer shows how Argentine psychoanalysis has been impacted by militant political struggles for gender equality in her country, and illustrates the relationship between subjectivity and power in the work of two prominent Argentine psychoanalysts, Silvia Bleichmar and Gilou García Reynoso."

Nancy Caro Hollander, *Ph.D., Research Psychoanalyst; Member of Psychoanalytic Institute of Northern California; Faculty of NYU Post-Doctoral Program in Psychotherapy and Psychoanalysis; Professor Emerita of History, California State University; Member and Past President of Psychoanalysis for Social Responsibility, Division 39 of the American Psychological Association; and Author of* Uprooted Minds: A Social Psychoanalysis for Precarious Times (Routledge, 2023)

"In this excellent book, *Post-patriarchal, Post-heteronormative, and Post-colonial Psychoanalysis: Psychoanalysis for All*, Debora Tajer offers a deep dive into theoretical and clinical issues from a psychoanalytic and gender perspective. The implications for our understanding of changing femininities and masculinities, new family and relationship configurations and changes in sexualities and gender identities are explored. It considers socio-historical changes, particularly since the fourth wave of feminist empowerment in the last decade. This book is important for the psychoanalytic clinician entering contemporary clinical scenarios. It will be an enrichment for readers interested in this crucial topic."

Patricia Alkolombre, *Ph.D., President and Chair of Women and Psychoanalysis Committee, International Psychoanalytic Association, COWAP IPA*

"In this remarkable book, Débora Tajer introduces her thoughts on gender and diversity, changes in family organization, trans-infancy as well as in the feminine condition and masculinity. Beyond traditional thinking, the author focuses on a clinical perspective facing the need to make transformations of the psychoanalytical approach to those changes. On this journey she proposes that contemporary psychoanalysis should be able to understand diverse subjectivities in order to contribute to a better theoretic-clinical comprehension of those that do not correspond to heterosexual and patriarchal norms. I highly recommend this book to psychoanalysts and other readers interested in this topic."

Leticia Glocer Fiorini, *Current Chair of the "Sexual and Gender Diversity Studies Committee" of the International Psychoanalytic Association (IPA) and Former President of the Argentine Psychoanalytical Association*

"If there is a future for psychoanalysis, it entails a work of depatriarchalization, deheterosexualization, and decolonization, as Paul B. Preciado stated. This is exemplified by Debora Tajer's inspiring non-hegemonic theory of gender. From the supposedly peripheral position of an Argentinean thinker, here emerges a revitalized psychoanalysis."

Patricia Gherovici, *Ph.D., Psychoanalyst and Author* of Transgender Psychoanalysis. A Lacanian Perspective on Sexual Difference

"Debora Tajer's book *Post-patriarchal, Post-heteronormative and Postcolonial Psychoanalysis: Psychoanalysis for All* is a wonderfully refreshing contribution to the intersectional renovation of psychoanalysis from Global South Feminist perspective, an approach mainstream psychoanalysis cruelly lacks. Not only does the author unveil the patriarchal, heteronormative and colonial vision underlying the 'classical' psychoanalytical approaches, but she also offers invaluable theoretical and clinical tools to apprehend the changes in feminities, masculinities, and gender identities, together with the new forms of sexual and affective relationships. I firmly believe there is a real need or this visionary book, as far as a political conception of psychoanalysis is concerned."

Thamy Ayouch, *Senior Lecturer (Professeur des Universités), Head of Master 2 "Psychoanalysis and Interdisciplinarity", Co-manager of the "Subject and social transformations" Axis of the CRPMS Laboratory, and Head of the "Gender Practices: Psychoanalysis, Medicine Education and Society" Degree Course*

"*Psychoanalysis for All* is a much-needed contribution to our psychoanalytic lexicon, and a timely and fresh toolbox to trace the haunting presence of patriarchy in contemporary psychoanalytic listening. Committed to the transmission of a psychoanalysis implicated in its political and historical drifts, Tajer generously shares the lessons learned from decades of work and makes the rich tradition of the 'Argentinean School of Psychoanalysis and Gender' available to an English-speaking audience. The book challenges us to re-think the clinic from the South, to the rhythm of a 'queer tango'. It is certainly a must-read!"

Dr. Tomás Ojeda, *Research in LGBTIQ+ Mental Health, Diversity Work, and Anti-gender Politics, and Trained Psychotherapist*

Contents

About the English Version

I would first of all like to thank Jorge Reitter who, by asking me to write the endorsement for his book *Oedipus Gay* in English, awakened in me the motivation to translate mine. I am also grateful to him for the contact with Routledge Publishers.

To Susannah Frearson and Saloni Singhania of Routledge for their assistance in editing this version.

To Jane Brodie for her excellent translation, which allowed me to translate my ideas into English.

To Rocio Fabbio for her assistance and support.

To Diego Baracat, librarian of the Asociación Psicoanalítica Argentina, for his support in translating the names and quotations of Sigmund Freud's books.

To Agustina Saudibet for her enthusiasm and encouragement to be translated.

To Patricia Porchat, Patricia Alkolombre, Thamy Ayouch, Nancy Caro Hollander, Leticia Glocer, Erica Burman, Jorge Reitter, Patricia Gherovici, and Tomás Ojeda for their wonderful endorsements.

And to Patricia Gherovici and Tomás Ojeda, in their capacity as bilingual psychoanalysts, for their cooperation in improving the translation of specific terms for a better and up-to-date translation for the English-speaking reader.

I would also like to thank to Diego Lorenzo and Mercedes Castruccio and the Programa Sur de apoyo a las traducciones of The Dirección General de Asuntos Culturales de la Cancillería de la República Argentina, for supporting the dissemination of Argentine cultural and academic production in the world.

Buenos Aires
June 2024

Introduction

This book recounts the difficulties encountered in attempting to construct theoretical-practical psychoanalytic tools for a post-patriarchal, post-heteronormative, and postcolonial perspective on human suffering.

Its strategy is twofold: first, to make visible the marks of patriarchy, heteronormativity, and coloniality underlying classic psychoanalytic perspectives, and, second, to provide the psychoanalytic community with the theoretical-clinical instruments acquired thus far by the currents of the discipline that have for some time brought a gender perspective to bear on psychoanalysis.

These perspectives are, I believe, both interesting and important to discerning the challenges facing clinical psychoanalysis today, specifically regarding changes in femininities and masculinities, the new configurations of relationships, current forms of employment and insertion in the labour market, and the new ideals constituted around these practices and social realities. At play are changes in how gender identities are assumed as well as how sexual desire and/or love is expressed.

This work also hopes to identify the clinical effects of the social legitimisation of other forms of sex and gender identity pursuant to the enactment of laws recognising same-sex marriage[1] and the right to decide one's own gender identity.[2]

Chapter 1 attempts to facilitate an understanding of the interrelationships between different gender ideals as socio-historical constructs and subjects' processes of singularisation and constitution of the psyche in the framework of those ideals. Chapter 2 re-examines psychoanalysis's conceptions of family and ideals of childrearing. It also presents contemporary works with a gender perspective on new family configurations and the specific theoretical and clinical tools those works have provided. Chapter 3 attempts to systematise the various contributions that psychoanalysis from a gender perspective has made to psychoanalysis in general. Chapter 4 discusses the experiences of trans children and how to understand and support them. Chapter 5 addresses clinical treatment of men from a gender perspective that attempts to deconstruct the hegemonic notions of masculinity they incorporated in their processes of subjectivation. That chapter discusses how the exercise of power causes harm not only to others but also to the men who engage in it. Chapter 6, which is not included in the Spanish edition, presents clinical experiences with women who have expanded their sexuality beyond heteronormative practices but who, with their male partners, face power conflicts of both an affective and sexual nature due to the tense coexistence of traditional and innovative relationship models.

Chapter 7 re-examines the relationship between subjectivity and power on the basis of the thinking of Silvia Bleichmar, an important Argentine psychoanalyst who did her doctoral work in psychoanalysis under Jean Laplanche. Chapter 8 furthers that line of reflection on the basis of the work of another major psychoanalyst, Franco-Argentine Gilou García Reynoso. I am personally grateful to them both: I attended Silvia Bleichmar's seminars for ten years, an experience that put before me a contemporary psychoanalysis that had re-examined the modernity at its roots to be able to speak of the present; it was in my 20-year treatment with Gilou García Reynoso that I was able to trace the marks on my own psyche of having become a subject in a patriarchal society—a process that afforded me the tools to accompany my patients on similar journeys. Chapter 9 includes a debate with fellow psychoanalysts of different tendencies who are just beginning to engage the dialogues between psychoanalysis and gender studies. The contents of that chapter stem from classes and exchanges at a number of psychoanalytic institutions to which I have been invited to discuss these issues. The chapter places emphasis on the need for interdisciplinary readings to avoid self-imposed isolation in what has been said and written thus far in the field of psychoanalysis: New realities must be tackled in all their specificity.

Throughout this book, the contributions of Ana María Fernández and Irene Meler, two enormous figures at the Escuela Argentina de Psicoanálisis y Género, make themselves felt. I am honoured to have studied and worked with them both over the years. The tools in psychoanalysis and gender that they provided me with is what allowed me to develop my own work.

I would like to thank my colleagues Graciela Reid and Alejandra Lo Russo for their contributions to late drafts of this text. I am grateful to Lucía Saavedra for her work as a research assistant and proofreader, and to Alejandro Vainer for his careful work as the editor of this book.

I would like to clarify what I mean when I say "the marks of patriarchy, heteronormativity, and coloniality" in psychoanalysis today and what I mean when I call for a post-patriarchal, postcolonial, and post-heteronormative vision. What follows are examples of each of those concepts:

1 Post-patriarchal: Identifying the still pertinent concepts bound to historical and hierarchical modes of relationships between the genders. Examples include (a) the theory of the father tied to males' having a monopoly on the symbolic function under patriarchy; (b) theories of femininity where

the desire to have a child is tied to the idea of making up for a lack and the notion that women have no other means to transcendence; and (c) motherhood equated with normal and fulfilled femininity.

A post-patriarchal vision identifies the marks of patriarchy in theory and practice to construct ideas and clinical interventions that do not direct subjects back to that which they have decided to reject, a source of additional suffering due to processes that establish inequality.

2 Post-heteronormative: Re-examining a binary conception of sexuality in which there are only two positions, whether or not tied to certain categories of biological bodies. At stake is fully recognising that the drive does not have an object a priori, which means that heterosexuality is not necessarily the most mature or healthy expression of sexuality. No less important is understanding how the biopolitical device of regulating sexualities as "legitimate" and "illegitimate" operates psychically by, for instance, "closeting" certain sexualities with the resulting malaise, an extra suffering that can by no means be attributed to intra-psychic dynamics. Identifying the forms of sexuality, affect, and family construction associated with sexual and gender-identity dissidence.

3 Postcolonial: Going beyond the collective sexual theory that holds that both children[3] and psychoanalysis come from Paris, as before they came from London or Vienna. Joking aside, I believe it is important to read and study psychoanalytic production from central countries in an off-centre fashion. A more horizonal exchange between production from different countries throws off the idea that there is a universal, when all that is a generalisation of the experiences of hegemonic subjects—that is, wealthy, white, heterosexual subjects from central countries. It is, in my view, important to draw on local production, in my case the production of a very active and prolific psychoanalytic community in Argentina. There is a need to produce theory grounded in located experiences. I believe it is important to produce theory according to one's own realities and that its value for other realities is given by having managed to "paint" one's own village, giving light to what happens in "other villages." Four examples related to gender include (a) a law that grants individuals the right to determine their own gender identity rather than force them "to rectify" what is seen as a psychopathology (that pathologising vision informs the legal framework in countries); (b) the Marriage Equality Act, which includes parenting rights. Local psychoanalysts played a very positive role in helping get that law passed, a far cry from the shameful position of their counterparts in other countries; (c) the feminist movement in Argentina, with its unique tradition. The Encuentros Nacionales de Mujeres have been held for 36 years straight; we invented the #NiUnaMenos movement to combat violence against women, a movement that later spread internationally; the enactment of a law legalising abortion free of charge at public hospital was passed in 2020, thanks

to a wave of activism that exceeded all expectations; and (d) Argentine psychoanalysis has a glorious tradition worth passing down and putting to work. The Asociación Psicoanalítica Argentina was founded in 1941, and since the 1950s psychoanalysts have worked in the public health system. Pursuant to political ruptures within the Argentine psychoanalytic community in the 1970s at the hands of movements known as Plataforma and Documento, it became possible to practise psychoanalysis outside the official institutions of the discipline. That freedom was what made possible the institution known as the Escuela Argentina de Psicoanálisis y Género.

My purpose is making from all this, an intersectional psychoanalysis, which takes into account the identity diversities even within each subject from a hybridity perspective (Ayouch, 2020).

For all those reasons, I invite you to read this book by someone who considers herself a trans (disciplinary) psychoanalyst. From the beginning of my career, my training and practice have encompassed clinical work, education, and research at the juncture between psychoanalysis, gender studies, and community health. In this book, you will find an approach that joins theory and clinical practice seen as a powerful whole rather than as two deficit parts.

What I offer you, then, is—I hope—a contribution to a propositional psychoanalysis that has re-examined the marks of patriarchy, heteronormativity, and coloniality that it bears.

Notes

1 Law enacted in Argentina in 2010.
2 Law enacted in Argentina in 2012.
3 Metaphor commonly used in Argentina to hide the sexual origin of procreation from children. It refers to the fact that historically the upper class made their honeymoons in Paris and returned to the country with pregnancies.

Reference

Ayouch, T. (2020) *Psicoanálisis e hibridez. Genero, colonialidad, subjetivaciones*. Ediciones Navarra Unbevú, México

Chapter 1

Gender and Subjectivation
Ways of Living, Loving, and Working

Organisation of the Experience of Life in Modernity: Public Men and Private Women

This chapter addresses the modern project's[1] production of gendered subjectivity around certain models of femininity and masculinity. The specific social needs associated with that project required a certain type of subjectivity, and in that framework subjects have engaged in individual processes of singularisation.

A correlate of the migration from the countryside to the city in order to work in factories or workshops was a novel mode of family life: the nuclear family (father, mother, and children, and no one else, living under the same roof).

The factory model required a strong labour force. Working-age males had to take an interest in performing tasks that compelled them to spend the whole day outside their habitational units selling their labour for wages. Women would be at the rearguard, performing domestic work and raising children. Over time, these socially assigned roles constituted ways of life; femineity and masculinity were constructed and, with them, gender ideals that subjects assumed for themselves and expected of others.

Thus, the figures of the public man and the private woman were constructed in a hierarchical relationship tied to a patriarchal society. With money as supreme value, wage labour afforded more power and autonomy than domestic labour and, as such, autonomy was a trait of the experience of men. Men could move from place to place, choose a vocation, and make decisions regarding purchases or investments. Women at the rearguard, meanwhile, would tend to men and "lick their wounds". Though the rearguard may have been invisible, without it the model would not have been viable. Early feminism's' aspiration to autonomy was never fulfilled, or not as fully as hoped for, and that has led to countless misunderstandings and disappointments. Only more recently has emphasis been placed on redistribution within the care economy for the sake of greater gender equity, thus questioning the autonomy/rearguard model.

DOI: 10.4324/9781003411253-1

At the dawn of the twenty-first century and in the wake of the 2001 economic, social, political, and institutional crisis[2] in Argentina, the labour insertion of both genders altered. While income inequality persisted as did unequal distribution of care tasks, there was greater and greater awareness of those inequalities. Those years witnessed the expansion of rights, including the enactment of same-sex marriage in 2010. The #NiUnaMenos' movement,[3] debates on the legalisation of abortion that culminated with its enactment in 2020, the reporting of abuse, and *escraches* (public shaming practices) against perpetrators of sex crimes have shaken up gender relations. Today, a range of novel modes of relationship exists alongside more traditional models.

Insofar as social imperatives and ideals inform the constitution of psyches, we can now see the impact that those historical changes have had on modes of subjectivation.

The term **mode of subjectivation** designates the articulation between the external and the internal, the macro and the micro. It refers to the conceptual construct at play in the back-and-forth between the forms of representation that each society enables for the conformation of subjects deemed apt to operate within that society, on the one hand, and how each subject constitutes their own singularity, on the other.

Social imperatives around gender along with asymmetrical power relations between men and women create submission and dispossessedness on the part of women who in turn develop specific forms of libidinal circulation and narcissism. In other words, those imperatives and power relations inform how affects and desires are developed and the models by which subjects constitute their identity and self-esteem. It is no less true that males' greater access to social and relational power generates a distinct set of styles. Significantly, these models have taken shape in a heteronormative framework based on the social need for biological reproduction and the aspiration of complementarity between the feminine and the masculine.

Gendered Modes of Subjectivation

It is not possible to speak of a single mode of gender subjectivation since relationships and social expectations around gender have been changing vertiginously since the mid-twentieth century. Variations in the system of gender relations can be tied to the production of specific modes of subjectivation.

The "baseline" modes of femineity form part of what is called a traditional model (Meler, 1994). In it, the feminine typology is tied to modernity's sexual division of labour as described above: women-mothers at the rearguard, that is, at home tending to the domestic space; and male workers performing wage labour in the public space.

The Feminine Gender

The **traditional mode of feminine gender subjectivation** describes how women structured their lives under modernity, mainly around the notion that motherhood and marriage were fundamental to their vital development. The feminine life project did not include vocational or professional development which, until around the middle of the twentieth century, was the sole terrain of men. Some authors (Larguía and Domoulin, 1988) have underscored the economic justification for this arrangement. They point out that love is what was supposed to make (traditional) women willing to turn the wages brought home by men into cooked food, a clean house, childrearing, and care services. In return, they expected that men represent them in the public space, support them economically, and protect them from the trials and dangers of, among other things, economic and political life. At stake in that traditional model is an asymmetrical division of roles and power where men enjoy more options and prerogative but are also expected to provide for the home in both economic and symbolic terms. How successful men are in the public sphere will determine the social status they are able to obtain for themselves and, by extension, for their families.

The groundwork for these roles based on the sexual division of labour is an asymmetrical division of power. The public space of wage labour and the social representation assigned to men is **a space where the power accumulated is more valuable in both social and relational terms than the "power of affects"** women can, perhaps, accumulate.

At the same time, the traditional model of the domestic and sentimentalised woman does not encompass the lived experience of all women under modernity. It is, rather, a **hegemonic representation that has had a major impact on the formation of an ideal of womanhood**.

As mentioned above, these notions have yielded specific mode of libidinal circulation and of narcissism. This analysis of the impact of social forms on the constitution of the psyche will revolve around the following: libidinal circulation (the sex and aggression drive), the conformation of a system of ideals, narcissistic structuration, the abilities of the ego, and the representation of one's own body.

Regarding libidinal circulation, women living under this modern model tend to express their **aggression** indirectly because, from a very young age, that drive is inhibited by mandates related to submission. In other words, as girls they learn that **only the powerful can express their anger openly, and that they do not have any power**. They have been brought up to be "good little girls", to be obedient and not make a fuss, and to be meek and speak in a soft voice or not to speak at all—those are the attributes of femineity. Those mandates establish privileged channels for the expression of aggression and complicate its management when girls grow up.

The resulting developmental difficulties include stunted expression of aggression (Burin, 1987), which takes the shape of failure to fully differentiate between themselves and others. Their relationships are characterised by fusion or the inability to recognise differences because of largely pre-Oedipal ties. Another difficulty is limited maturation of socially sanctioned forms of expressing differences in position vis-à-vis others. That means they often express themselves in an explosive fashion that generates rejection and, thus, often go unheard.

This stymied circulation leads to other difficulties: women turning against themselves (masochism), and the indirect or "poisonous" expression of aggressive feelings, or their indiscriminate expression because of the failure to tie representation and affect. In other words, women operating in this model express their anger after the fact and in an explosive fashion due to its accumulation. That, in turn, perplexes the people on the receiving end of that expression.

At the same time, the expression of sexuality is neither active nor direct but passive and repressed—that because of the social mandate that a "good woman" not express her sexual desire openly but react "passively" to expressions of male desire directed at her. That social norm was designed to assure legitimate offspring, that is, that women specifically not have children out of wedlock. At play is a double sexual standard for men and women in modernity: the naturalised idea of unbridled male sexuality enables them, as the powerful group, to have sex with whomever they want, while their wives "naturally" desire their husbands and only their husbands.

Eroticism that is not expressed directly often produces neurotic or corporal symptoms. Relationships with men tend to become tender and "maternal", and the mother-child tie eroticised. Indeed, eroticism is reduced to the function of conception.

This double standard informs how women, or at least women of a certain type living under the modern model, respond to infidelity on the part of their partners. They have been encouraged to value the persistence of their relationship and their status as a married woman above all else. After all, losing it could have serious implications for their social and economic position.

In these women's value system, motherhood and marriage based on feminine faithfulness and honour reign supreme. Their personal fulfilment in other spheres is secondary. These women only work for pay if necessary to help support the family. Otherwise, they do not work outside the home. After all, such work does not correspond to the images that bolster their self-worth or their worth in society. Of paramount importance to these women's self-esteem is choosing "a good husband"—that is, a successful husband who is a hard worker as well as a good father. They themselves are a "good catch" insofar as beautiful in youth and good mothers and housewives later on. Much of these women's sense of self-worth depends on their successful performance in the roles of mother and housewife. Marital arrangements are based on asymmetrical and complementary roles; "separate worlds" ("Don't worry about that, that's my area") keep latent conflicts from coming to the surface. When marital conflicts do arise, the husbands tend to use tools, including humiliation, that reaffirm the hierarchical difference between themselves and their wife.

Their skills as housewives and as mothers are honed; they are neat, orderly, and empathetic. But their development in the public world is stunted and their abilities weak; their autonomy is limited in that sphere except when they work as "secretaries reporting to a superior" or for their spouses. They have social skill when it comes to affective ties but are awkward when it comes to the codes of the public world because those codes have not formed part of their process of subjectivation. This is evident, for instance, in their handling of labour contracts and agreements in general, in their negotiation of financial questions, and in their participation in meetings other than those strictly necessary meetings where relationships beneficial to advancement at work are often established.

Their representation of their own body is linked to ideals of beauty and youth. Attention to one's body is, for these women, fundamental; their power resides in being young and beautiful and, thus, being chosen for marriage. Yet they fail to appropriate their bodies. After all, their bodies are there to please others. The consequences of this for their health can be serious, since self-care is not a priority.

Transitional Modes of Feminine Subjectivation

The changes that took place starting in the second half of the twentieth century when women began entering the workforce—gradually, but on a mass scale—and, relatedly, higher levels of formal education produced what might be called a **transitional** mode of **feminine subjectivation.** These women enthusiastically entered the public world on a mass scale, but they still harboured within the traditional woman=wife model, a social mandate that was now coupled with vocational and professional demands. In these women's love relationships with men,[4] the expectation is still that the man be the primary provider on economic and symbolic levels. In the family and relationship sphere, then, the man's professional development is the priority, often to the detriment of the woman's. Though less extreme than in the traditional model, in this one as well control remains in the hands of the man.

Regarding drives, this model is characterised by competitiveness and rivalry. Conflicts tend to be poorly managed, though not avoided despite long discussion to that end. These women's vision of themselves is often aggressive, that is, tending to masochism and depression; they are frequently ridden with guilt. That aggressivity is often indiscriminate and, as such, seems arbitrary. Aggression takes the form of resentment and envy, usually directed at the woman's life partner partly because he is the one closest at hand and partly in retaliation for the power asymmetry. Resentment and envy can, however, be expressed as jealousy, dissatisfaction, and endless demands.

Eroticism in marriage is valued and sexual pleasure deemed important. Notwithstanding, because the double standard of the traditional model persists, the possibility that the husband has extramarital relationship is met with resentment. In some cases, women would like to enjoy that same possibility, but they do not because their self-esteem is based to the values of "female honor" and faithfulness even when those values are not reciprocal.

Eroticism is, at times, transformed into tenderness. But in the case of these women, unlike those living under the traditional model, that transformation is cause for conflict: they are not able to consummate the erotic tie they so value and desire.

The core values in the system of ideals at play in this transitional mode are motherhood and marriage, but they are combined with expectations for satisfaction in the public world, even if that is a secondary value. These women tend to value and desire powerful and successful men even as they fear or are wary of them. After all, they do not want to feel lesser than their partners. That attraction to dominant males despite their ideals is the result of the persistence of the asymmetrical power distribution between men and women in the constitution of the psyche. In other words, it is an effect of the internalisation of patriarchy, which is by no means a thing of the past, and its model of heterosexuality. For those reasons, they often denigrate the partner they "were able to catch" when he fails to satisfy the hegemonic ideals of masculine triumph. What arises is competition with their partners on matters of success and/or autonomy. These women are rife with contradictions. On the one hand, they want to get a topnotch man to take care of and serve, and, on the other, they feel envy that that other is in a situation they would want for themselves. To make matters worse, they tend to disdain men who are not particularly dominant.

Their skills as homemakers and as mothers are instrumental; they are more geared to resolving domestic issues than concerned with making sure everything is picture-perfect. They often apply the logic of the private sphere to the public world, which is an obstacle when it comes to contractual agreements and hierarchical relationships; their workplace relationships become a question of affect. They have trouble negotiating remuneration for their work and often wait for others to set wages or fees for them only to then get angry when they deem that compensation unfair. They expect to be treated well because beloved rather than because efficient or efficacious. They are competitive with other women and tend to overestimate men. They don't understand the need to be diplomatic because not well versed in the codes of the public space even when they have operated in it for years. They often believe they can take care of everything themselves and harbour strict ideas of righteousness, but have trouble delegating and organising tasks.

Regarding the body, these women pay less attention than their counterparts in the traditional model to the ideals of beauty linked to their social value as women and their ability to find a spouse. That said, a youthful body is a value and cause for competition with other women, which has intensified in general in recent times. One term of their unwritten marital contracts is caring for their bodies; the expectation is that they stay fit and youthful—indeed, that is more important than an appropriation of their own bodies for the sake of their own pleasure. Be that as it may, there are more and more representations tied to a notion of personal pleasure in the body—something entirely absent in the more traditional model.

Innovative Modes of Feminine Subjectivation

The dawn of the twenty-first century witnessed **novel modes of feminine gender subjectivation**, which are hard to categorise because so diverse. One unifying characteristic in the novel construction of the feminine subject, however, is an understanding of motherhood and marriage as a choice, rather than as an unquestionable mandate or constituent part of femineity. Work in the labour market under conditions that vary according to social sector is, of course, a requirement for women who support themselves, as this group of women does, whether they live alone, with their life partners, or with their families.

While these women do not shy away from competition, they are less antagonistic than the women in the previous groups because of a formal or strategic style that enables objectives to be reached in a more deliberate fashion. That is possible, thanks to instrumental or operative expressions of aggression where what they feel corresponds to what they express. In other words, they are able to convey in a more measured and logical way what angers them to the ones who anger them.

They are better able to express their erotic desires. They distinguish between practises aimed at obtaining erotic pleasure and practises aimed at establishing a lasting relationship, which means they need not be in love with a partner to enjoy a sexual relation with him or her—a near impossibility in the models of femininity where being in love is a prerequisite for sex.

Their self-esteem is based on the ideals of work as well as motherhood. More and more women are either putting off motherhood for until after their careers have reached a certain level or opting not to have children at all—a novelty since for the other two groups of women childlessness is seen as a cruel fate rather than a valid choice. This is also the first group of women that chooses to raise children without a partner rather than doing so as a result of abandonment on the part of the other biological parent.

But there is an underside to this greater degree of freedom and lesser degree of external coercion: they are faced with the need to make decisions when women have, until recently, been used to obeying and enduring. As a gender, they have little experience in responsibility as subjects and in autonomy when they have accumulated some measure of power.

As a result, they bear the weight of two or more very demanding ideals (being excellent mothers, wonderful partners, and remarkable workers, for instance) in a still patriarchal world. It is often difficult for them to give up on any of those demanding ideals even partly or to curb their aspirations and ambitions for the sake of balancing the different desires they harbour or possibilities they enjoy.

Skill at that balancing act is indispensable in the face of a historical juncture that upholds a demanding model of success, the aspiration to a "full life" despite continued inequity in the distribution of childrearing and domestic work. The coexistence of those antagonist ideals condemns these women to an overdemanding inner life and life in the world: even highly successful women often feel like failures.

They often suffer a narcissistic collapse due to the dimensions of the goals they set. After all, the system of ideals they grapple with is not only more complex than the one at play in the other two models but also rife with contradictions.

Notwithstanding, their self-esteem is higher than the women who live under the traditional model, whether from the same generation or earlier ones, because they have more power in the public world and in their relationships.

In terms of their skills, these women develop domestic-expressive skills as well as workplace-instrumental skills; that is, certain traditional skills are not eschewed as new ones associated with their new roles are embraced. The women in this group who were raised according to a model that privileges the public sphere tend to have stunted expressive skills; they were brought up to inhibit affectivity and its expression for the sake of success in the public sphere.

They appropriate their bodies more fully as source of pleasure than their counterparts in the other models; its sole value is not as object of beauty. Though there are variations according largely to social class, this group of women works out with a certain frequency for reasons of health and beauty; their routines vary with the needs and possibilities of each moment in the life cycle. Many are very conscious of both their diets and the environment, which explains in part the enormous recent growth in the number of naturalists, vegetarians, and vegans.

The Masculine Gender

Traditional Mode

The term "traditional mode of masculine gender subjectivation" refers to men who have structured their life around values like being the provider and breadwinner for their families. Their identity and vitality are geared to the public world (work, politics, clubs, institutions, and so forth). Given the asymmetry of gender roles and the relative power of the two genders, these men have more life options and greater prerogative than women. At stake in the traditional mode of masculine subjectivation and its construction is domination and the exercise of power—and that has myriad effects on these men's daily lives and relationships.

In terms of love relationships, the asymmetry in power relationships is connected to the sexual double standard of the sort described above. Those who benefit from the traditional model have the privilege of structuring their sexuality in a broader field than their female counterparts. They draw a distinction between "good" women to marry and "bad" women with whom to take sexual pleasure.

This model of masculinity is tied to the needs of industrial society, among them the promise of an economic surplus to compensate one's life partner and family for the extended absence from the home during the workday. In other words, providing for the family economically is a form of symbolic compensation men provide to make up for their unavailability; because they are at work, they are unavailable for tasks such as caring for the sick, attending school assemblies, and doing housework.

As we have seen, one of the effects of gendered social mandates based on asymmetrical power relations between men and women is granting men the prerogative of masculine hegemony. Men's libidinal circulation is wider than women's, and at play in their narcissism are other contents and values.

They are authorised to experience and express the aggression drive when the prerogatives of the traditional masculine role go unsatisfied, prerogatives tied to domination and greater valorisation of their social role compared to those of subaltern subjects (women, children, and subordinates at work or on the social scale). That aggression drive is also at play, and deemed legitimate, in their relationships with male peers or those higher up in the hierarchy, though in those situations that drive is reined in out of fear of negative consequences. Aggression is used instrumentally to get what they want, and the use of violence is considered legitimate as a last resort in a situation where their status or social image is undermined or challenged. They value the ability to control themselves when they get angry.[5] They often cover up or deny the existence of conflicts in their close relationships because their mode of subjectivation has provided them with limited tools to work through conflicts or express what they feel. Rivalry is commonplace; they anger easily and often, mostly as an effect of subjectivation for domination. At the same time, they rarely realise the damage their actions and words cause others, which is why many of these men are scared of losing control of the situation and the possible outcomes of that loss of control. Competition is important as a means to bolster a self-image tied to meeting goals.

Singularisation, that is, differentiation from others, is based on the constant use of the word "no" and on physical and emotional distance.

They are characterised by a marked dissociation between erotism and tenderness, though that does not seem to irk them[6] since, as indicated above, women are divided into the "good" ones to marry and the "bad" ones with whom to enjoy sex. They expect their wives or life partners to treat them with maternal tenderness, though in more recent times they have started to be bothered by the cost of such arrangements. After all, they want not only to be coddled but also to be desired by their partners—and that is off the table in extremely maternal relationships.

Genital sex is associated with abasement of the erotic object ("I hope she is a whore in bed"). Partial drives are released without any restraint, and fantasies tend to be tied to boundless domination of the sex scene. Having parallel sexual relationships is tied to men's right to dominate women, a right that traditional males covet; they react negatively to a proposal of symmetry on the part of the women they have chosen as wives or life partners. Relatedly, men in the traditional model have, historically, been indifferent to whether their partners derive sexual pleasure from their encounters; they consider them a sort of "loving repository" of male eroticism. That situation, though, is beginning to change as expectations about sexual pleasure in marriage vary.

Their self-esteem is based on self-mastery (Foucault, 1986) and discipline in the moral and intellectual spheres, and the power to procreate (Fuller, 2000), as well as having triumphed in at least one area of life.

To be a "good man" for these traditional male subjects is tied to the image of the worker and the provider, to earning respect and getting ahead in life. When faced with wrenching social situations or conflicts in their relationships, they often feel that their "masculinity is threatened"—that because they tend to equate their personal identity with their gender identity. For that reason, a threat to the values around which their identity is built is often experienced as a threat to their masculinity. In situations where they perceive their masculinity as under threat, they tend to defend themselves by reaffirming their virility through domination. Mechanisms include the denigration of others in general and of women in particular; they can even take the form of violence.

From a very young age, they are encouraged to master themselves in order to then master others (Foucault, 1986).[7] As a consequence, they are unskilled at expressing emotion (as the saying goes, "real men don't cry"). Sociability tends to ensue at the workplace or modernity's venues for masculine social life (at the club and around sports or politics) in which women do not participate (Tajer, 1998). The key values in those ties to other men are loyalty and shared interests. Social relationships outside work or the aforementioned venues are few. For that reason, workplace flexibilisation and remote work have taken away the privileged spaces in which male friendships are formed. They associate the quality of a friendship with its duration, and rarely make new friends ("friends forever" is a key value). They hold affect expressed through deeds over affect expressed through words. They do not perceive themselves as equal to women, and as a result their relationships with them are hierarchical or understood, at least by them, as a sort of guardianship. In other words, they take care of women when they love them or if those women are their responsibility, but they do not consider them peers with the same rights and obligations. As we shall see in Chapter 5, in sex in the context of a love relationship, they tend to take more than they give. After all, whether or not they see it, they are the ones with the "dominant" position in the "market".

They are alienated from their bodies and protect themselves in the face of an intrusion or the fear that the other, regardless of sex, get "under their skin". The effects of that alienation include the sensation of "otherness" in relation to their bodies that prove an obstacle to self-care and caring for others[8]; they are slow to get the medical care they require.

Their image of virility is tied to taking physical risks, which leads to accidents and excesses and to the failure to detect fatigue. They see their bodies as "high-performance machines" that meet the production needs of modernity and their own needs to see themselves as "tough guys" (Bonino Méndez, 1998). At the same time, physical activity forms part of the construction of the masculine body in this model. Workout routines vary with social position and age (García, 2001). Working-class traditional males, for instance, associate physical activity and sports with their youth, and they stop working out when they get married; their more affluent counterparts, meanwhile, keep playing sports like football (soccer) or tennis—perhaps golf as they get older—and working out at the gym regardless of age or marital status.

Transitional Modes of Masculine Subjectivation

Some more modern men participate in transitional modes of masculine subjectivation. A more equal relationship with women is one of their expectations for adult life. An empirical observation that does not aspire to generalisation shows that men in this transitional model have a close relationship to their mothers when growing up and that they do not deny that relationship as the price to pay for the privileged of adult masculinity. These men identify and empathise with their mothers, and that enables them to valorise the intimate and the affective regardless of hegemonic masculinity.[9] They attempt to balance that valorisation with the skills and mandates of public masculinity—and that results in inner tension between tenderness and toughness.

In these transitional masculinities, then, components of the traditional model, like the idea of the public male who is a provider, exist alongside close affective ties in daily relationships with family and partners. Indeed, those ties are important to their personal development. The power distribution between the genders in this model is somewhat more equitable; male domination is attenuated, which mitigates male responsibility as a provider. They face new and multiple paradoxes as they attempt to coordinate different realms, projects, and models, whether in relation to their own lives or the lives of their partners.

Like their traditional counterparts, these men are authorised to feel and express aggression when others do not respect their prerogatives as men.

The difference in relation to those subjects is that these men connect to the pain the expression of aggression can inflict on the other. When, thanks to the expression of others, they understand that their attitude has caused harm, they try to reel it in and make up for that harm with empathy. Their aggression, then, is expressed in the naturalised habitat of masculine domination (Bourdieu, 1987, 1986); they themselves are blind to a mechanism of domination incorporated at such a young age.[10]

They are skilled at the instrumental use of aggression and can even resort to violence in extreme situations. At the same time, they value the ability to control aggression as a sign of maturity ("I was out of control when I was a kid"). While there is a tendency to deny conflicts in love relationship due to undeveloped skills at resolving them and at expressing emotions in general, it is less extreme than among their traditional counterparts. They are interested in competing, but they value process over results; they are less interested in upholding an impressive image of themselves than traditional men are, and that affords them greater autonomy vis-à-vis masculine gender ideals than those men. They allow themselves to be more like they are and less "the way a man should be".

In their sex lives, tenderness and eroticism are less divided than in the case of more traditional men, though they do expect mothering of some sort from their wives or life partners. At the same time, they value erotic pleasure, or at least the possibility of it, with their partner. A sexuality associated with degradation of the erotic object persists, but it is more attenuated and playful. They do not, for the most part, make a habit of having sex outside their primary relationship, but they do have "passing flings" when that relationship is faced with conflict or when opportunities arise (trips, conferences, and so forth). They understand that their partners might take the same liberties, but fervently hope that they do not. A double life is cause for conflict for this group of men because, unlike their traditional counterparts, sexual pleasure and love are somewhat connected. Besides, they empathise with the possible suffering such relationships could cause their partners whom, furthermore, they would not like to lose.

The ego ideal revolves around values like effort, willpower, and kindness. Self-esteem rests on the idea of being a good man, an image tied to values of work, being a provider, and earning respect in the professional sphere. Also important, however, is being someone loved for who they are, regardless of social status. At play is a search for balance between the public and private worlds.

Their self-esteem is not threatened by the demonstration of tenderness, and success is, for them, a relative value.

Like traditional men, they develop skills of self-mastery, but they are less afraid of, and more versed at, expressing their emotions. They talk about work with their friends and partners, but also share their emotions. They see being the primary breadwinner as their responsibility, though they value the fact that their wives work. Their friendships, mostly with men, are based on the values of loyalty, common interests, and work. With phrases like "there is no such thing as friendship between a man and a woman—there is always a hidden agenda" and "friendship between a man and a woman is for gays", they express the homophobia characteristic of hegemonic masculinity. They too always have to prove that they are not feminine, children, or homosexuals (Badinter, 1992).

They are more forgiving than traditional men (they value flexibility), and they form new friendships as their interests and affinities change over the years.

Regarding their relationship to their bodies, their notion of virility is tied to exposure to risk, excess, and not registering fatigue, but they also value self-care and looking good. Excess can sometimes take the form of compulsive exercise, in which they see their bodies as high-performing machines, though a more sophisticated one in the case of more affluent groups. Compulsive exercise can also be a defensive reaction against fear of ageing and the risk of illnesses it brings.

Innovative Modes of Masculinity

Finally, innovative modes of masculinity are diverse; they cannot be grouped under a specific typology. In that gambit, success in the public world, marriage, and fatherhood are options in the construction of the masculine subject rather than the requirements for it. These men are more and more skilled at taking care of themselves and of those they love in a logic of more democratic relations between genders and generations, as well as an ethics of care.

On an intra-psychic level, aggression and its expression are seen as legitimate, though there is a clear understanding of the danger that, if unbridled, that expression can turn into abuse. These men are more connected with the pain they can inflict and the pain they can experience.

They do not, generally speaking, fear losing control when they get angry. When faced with situations of competition, they choose whether to avoid or to engage according to the specifics of the situation. Rather than a clear dichotomy between winning and losing, they understand that there are situations where "you win by losing"—evidence of an identity less connected to an image of masculinity than to internal and personal values.

They value both eroticism and tenderness and are interested in bringing them together. Erotic pleasure in their primary relationship matters to them, and its absence can be cause of conflict or even separation. Genital sex is associated with a range of fantasies that are, in some cases, shared with their partners. Both members of the couple enjoy the same prerogative to have other relationships, sometimes as an occasional escape in times of conflict. These men believe that those extra-relationship encounters could hurt the relationship, and hence do not tell their primary partners about them unless they are ready to end the relationship. That said, there is, at the same time, growing interest—especially on the part of younger people—in open relationships, where what goes on with others is no secret even as the primary relationship is privileged. Another novel arrangement is polyamory, where there is no hierarchy between relationships. Time will tell how these arrangements evolve.

For these men, unlike those in the other groups, faithfulness is seen as a personal choice; it is tied to how in love or satisfied they are with their relationship. Significantly, male homosexuals were at the forefront of making faithfulness an explicit contract in a relationship rather than an assumption. The "lag" among heterosexual couples is because men rarely see women as political peers[11] in the field of sexuality. That is changing, though. In my clinical practise, I first came upon women proposing these alternative arrangements a few years ago. The women making the proposals had either had sexual experiences with other women or worked in and/or investigated the field of sexual diversity. More recently, though, the idea of not assuming exclusivity a priori has become slightly more widespread in relationships between men and women. Indeed, there is now a term in Spanish for the "non-exclusive" period of a relationship in formation, a phase during which the tie is primarily sexual: "*chonguear*". These different phases and arrangements have now made their way into the "hetero planet" on almost equal terms for men and women in what some have called the *queerification* of relationships in general.

Returning to the innovative men, the ideal they have structured encompasses the values of beauty and kindness alongside the more traditional value of being providers. They care about creativity and resist being alienated at work whenever possible; they refuse to accept alienation as a condition for existence, for being as men. In other words, their perception of themselves is not based on what they do; their identity is not embedded in work the way it is in the earlier models. The image of the good man is tied, for the most part, to personal values rather than gender expectations and prerogatives. Success is a relative value; what matters more to them is being able to incorporate feelings of tenderness into their everyday lives.

Emotional skills are important to them, and they try to cultivate those skills, hard though that may be because a value largely neglected in the constitution of masculinity under modernity. They talk about work and their relationships; they enjoy themselves with friends of both sexes and with their partners. They do not believe it is their responsibility to be the primary breadwinner. Their often very profound friendships with men and women are based on loyalty, shared interests, affect, and work. They are open to making new friends. They see themselves as capable of forgiving themselves and others.

They perceive their bodies as their own, and one of their ideals is caring for their body and its appearance. While, like the earlier models, this one is tied to risk, it is less extreme and offset by the value of exploration. They register feelings of fatigue and stop to rest. The machine image of the body in the earlier models exists alongside images tied to pleasure and play, in other words they lived experience of the body. The body forms part of their representation of themselves: they are, among other things, their bodies.

And Now What?

This chapter has introduced the different modes of feminine and masculine gender subjectivation that have arisen over time, but that also exist simultaneously, during the same historical period, albeit with specificities tied to generation, race, social class, and geographic location. Indeed, we could even say that the traditional, transitional, and innovative models coexist within a single subject and a single love relationship.

These models should not be understood as rigid. What I have attempted to lay out is a sort of schematic account of the relations between the macrosocial of the patriarchal system, on the one hand, and the construction of gendered subjectivities, on the other, even though those subjectivities are, of course, constantly changing.

In these times of new signifiers and experiences of sex and affect, we harbour within us a range of longings and understandings. Polyamory, the importance of consent, the notion that love is curse,[12] the possibility—in the case of women—of separating sex from love, and transits of identity and sex are just some of the facets and practises of current existence that have gained visibility and legitimacy. Like all changes, these produce new pleasures as well as new malaises—freedom comes at an often-wrenching cost. And there is not yet a guide to love.

Notes

1 In sociopolitical terms, the dawn of the modern age can be pegged to the French Revolution. In terms of labour, it began with the Industrial Revolution, which introduced the capitalist mode of production.
2 The uprising led then President Fernando de la Rúa to resign.
3 A movement that condemns and combats violence against women and LBGTQ* (lesbian, bisexual, gay, trans, queer and plus) people (2015).
4 This is fundamentally the case in sexual and love relationships between men and women due to gender asymmetry under patriarchy and its internalisation in processes of subjectivation. It also occurs in relationships between women, however, where there is a power asymmetry tied to a difference in socioeconomic status, age, nationality, ethnicity, or other categories that organise social asymmetry and that are internalised in the processes of subjectivation. Furthermore, modes of gender subjectivation should not be associated wholesale with choice of erotic object (the combinations of the two factors are multiple). I explain this in greater detail in Chapter 6.
5 The valorisation of self-control in relation to the expression of anger varies with social sector. Very broadly speaking, men in middle and upper-middle social and cultural sectors value self-control more than their less affluent counterparts.

6 Many traditional men have no trouble dissociating their erotic life from their affective life or dividing them into two separate spheres. But when those two worlds intersect, conflicts arise and the male's strategies often prove inadequate, for example, a lover who wants more attention or gets pregnant, and the official partner or wife finds out.

7 This characteristic of traditional masculinity is more central and sophisticated in subjects either born to or who achieve higher socioeconomic levels.

8 An illustrating anecdote: an anesthesiologist who attend to one of my classes said that some "gender tools" would have come in handy in dealing with a male patient who did not want to be put under anesthesia so as not to avoid losing control of the situation. He did not trust that the other man, the doctor, would do him no harm once he was under.

9 A recent text by Benjamin (2022) casts a new light on this understanding. At stake is not only a close tie with the actual mother, but wholehearted appropriation of what is signified as feminine in patriarchal culture (tenderness, vulnerability, attachment, etc.). She argues that, in our culture, masculinity operates as a rejection of "feminine weakness", and toughness, that is, disconnect from one's own feelings of vulnerability, as a masculine defence before fear of fragmentation.

10 In other words, they can cause harm despite themselves because of the naturalisation of the exercise of power. The most empathetic of these men ask for forgiveness and try to patch things up once the harm they have caused has been brought to their attention.

11 "Political peers" in sex and love is a concept developed by Fernandez (2009). She understands political in the sense of distribution of power and includes it in the field of relationship. Here, I use the concept to indicate that in male/female love relationships one of the problems, even today, is that men do not see women as equals. I explain this concept in greater depth in Chapter 5.

12 It is, today, more acceptable on both social and subjective levels to manifest erotic desire than to be, or show oneself to be, in love. It is as if love had replaced sex as a taboo.

References

Badinter, E. (1992) *XY de L'Identité masculine*, Odile Jacob (ed.)

Benjamin (2022) Vulnerabilidad, repudio y violencia: la tragedia de la masculinidad, en Romano, A., Alkolombre, P. y Cardó, G. (comp.), *Poder, género y amor I perspectivas masculinas contemporáneas*, Letra viva

Bonino Méndez, L. (1998) Reconstruyendo la 'normalidad' masculina. Apuntes para una 'psicopatología' de género masculino, en *Actualidad Psicológica*, N° 253, Buenos Aires

Bourdieu, P. (1986) *Distinction*, Routledge

Bourdieu, P. (1987) *Choses dites*, Le Éditions de Minuit

Burin, M. (1987) *Estudios sobre la subjetividad femenina*, GEL

Fernandez, A.M. (2009) *Las lógicas sexuales* :amor, política y violencias,Nueva Visión

Fernandez, A.M. y Siqueira Peres, W. (comp.) (2013) *La Diferencia Desquiciada. Géneros y Diversidades Sexuales*, Biblos

Foucault, M. (1986) *The history of sexuality 3. The care of the Self*, Pantheon Books

Fuller, N. (2000) Significados y Prácticas de Paternidad entre Varones Urbanos del Perú, en Fuller, Norma (comp.), *Paternidades en América Latina*, Pontificia Universidad Católica del Perú

García, C.I. (2001) La pedagogía del cuerpo como bastión del género, en *Revista Nómadas*, N° 14

Larguía, I. y Domoulin, J. (1988) *La mujer nueva. Teoría y práctica de su emancipación*, Centro Editor de América Latina

Meler, I. (1994) Parejas de la transición. Entre la psicopatología y la respuesta creativa, en *Actualidad Psicológica, 214*, pp. 7–12, Buenos Aires

Tajer, D. (1998) El Fútbol como organizador de la masculinidad, en *Revista La Ventana*, N° 8, Buenos Aires

Chapter 2

The Modern Family Model

Contemporary Alternatives and New Challenges

The industrial revolution and the onset of modernity brought a number of changes to the daily life of subjects, among them the configuration of a new family unit: the nuclear family. That family—no more than two married adults (man and woman) and their biological offspring—was an effect of a number of changes that took place at that juncture. Very briefly, migration to the city from the countryside and life in those cities in smaller habitational units led to a change from extended families living under the same roof to cohabitation of smaller families of just two generations tied by blood as well as a social alliance.

This way of life produced a change in the relationship between patriarchy[1] and family life. The ties between men of the same lineage were democratised: One great patriarch of the entire kinship group was replaced by small patriarchs in the new nuclear family structure. One result of this mode of family life was the production of specific and historically located forms of masculinity and femininity, the ones described earlier in this book. In the late nineteenth century and within this now well-established socio-relational context, psychoanalysis arose. It considered the nuclear family model "the family"—the "natural" setting for the plots that would form the basis of psychoanalysis and its contributions to the constitution of the human psyche and sexuality.

By the time psychoanalysis had taken hold in the Rio de la Plata[2] (the 1940s and 1950s), a new ingredient was at play in the nuclear family: romance and romantic love. Later, in the 1960s and 1970s, the novel expectation of erotic pleasure within the marital bond was also brought into the picture.

A lot of water has passed under the bridge of family configurations since the 1940s. Regarding the family and other core concerns of psychoanalysis, we must consider Freud's work a point of departure, not of arrival (or dogma), and re-examine what has to be reworked in it to avoid becoming, even unwittingly, allies to the most conservative forces in society.

And that is no easy feat for psychoanalysis. The very crux of its corpus (notions like the oedipal complex, sexual difference, symbolic castration, and psycho-sexuality as a whole) is tied to the historically contingent nuclear family formation. Attempts to reformulate psychoanalysis often come up against

DOI: 10.4324/9781003411253-2

the wrenching question of what will remain of the discipline and of being psychoanalysed if we re-examine those central ideas.Refusing to ask this question for fear of the despair it provokes prevents us from responding to current challenges regarding the production of subjectivity or the nature of affective bonds

Like all human disciplines, psychoanalysis as we know it today bears the historical marks of the conditions in which it appeared. And, in that sense, we must distinguish which parts of it remain relevant and which do not because they remained tied to forms of knowledge, commonsense, and normalcy from another era.

The hypothesis of Juliet Mitchell's book *Psychoanalysis and Feminism* produced a dramatic shift in the relationship between feminism and psychoanalysis in the 1970s. Previously, mainstream feminism and the twentieth century left in general mistrusted that "bourgeois science"; it delivered "cures" that ended up reducing discontent with hegemonic culture to tolerable levels. Mitchell changed the focus, arguing that psychoanalysis can act as "a very good device to analyse the production of subjective suffering in bourgeois and patriarchal society, rather than just a means to reproduce that society". In keeping with that formulation, today's challenge is to explore whether we can turn the psychoanalytic corpus into an approach to human suffering in today's society that does not prop up subjects to return them to what is often seen as a lost balance but rather projects them into post-patriarchy, post-heteronormativity, and postcoloniality.

Our premise, then, is as simple as it is powerful when it comes to tackling today's needs: a re-examination of what was, for psychoanalysis, the normal and desirable family, the family structure at the root of most of its theoretical developments and clinical tools—that is, the nuclear family, the family of modernity. And, bearing that in mind, our interventions must creatively endeavour to do something other than uphold the status quo.

If we perform the arduous task of unpacking the nuclear family, we find that there are a number of objects of analysis:

- For many subjects, that family model has been and is more a social ideal or imaginary construction than a lived reality. Many modern subjects lived in large extended families or what are known today as diverse families.[3]
- The nuclear family model/ideal constitutes, to a large extent, expectations of happiness/unhappiness in late modernism.
- Since romantic love became the basis for marriage[4]—and that was not until the early twentieth century—marriage has become the institution that legitimises heterosexual love relationships; kinship is only recognised to the extent that it takes the form of direct family. That means that important ties that have no name in modernity's limited kinship system go unrecognised, which takes a particularly great toll at important junctures in life (Butler, 2004).

- The heterosexuality on which the nuclear family is based revolves around a division between public men and private women, but that is by no means the only possible form of heterosexuality.

Thus far, I have offered an account of what gender studies have been saying about the family for the last 50 years—nothing new for anyone working in that field, but quite a novelty for psychoanalytic theory and clinical practice. For that reason, it is still necessary to call attention to the ongoing effects of the modern family on everyday life and on clinical practice. In other words, the fact that these reflections are nothing new on the level of intellectual production does not mean they have been brought into current clinical devices. And I would venture to say that the novelty lies precisely in bringing these reflections to bear on the everyday practice of our fellow analysts.

And I believe that this is the moment to undertake that change in practice. A great many psychoanalysts are beginning to grasp the need to address the current modes of suffering of subjects who do not live in nuclear, patriarchal, or heteronormative family arrangements or aspire to live in them. Unfortunately, most psychoanalysts confront these challenges using theoretical-clinical tools that consider only patriarchal (and modern) modes of psyche organisation— they know no others. And therein lies one of the greatest contradictions in clinical practice today: One the one hand, there is widespread support for diversity; on the other, paternal dogma continues to operate, perhaps not explicitly, as model of normalcy everywhere, but especially in moments foundational to the formation of the psyche, that is, childrearing. This contradiction has given rise to what has come to be described as homophobia without homophobes, racism without racists, and patriarchy without sexists.

Towards a New Horizon: Family Life Today, the Production of Subjectivity, and Its Clinical Challenges

I would like to cite a passage that clearly expresses what underlies and orients the work of a gender approach to psychoanalysis:

> The Father [is] a historical construct, an ally of traditional forms of male domination that assure the male father a monopoly on the symbolic function. The end of the father, of the Western patriarchy, is the end of a world, not the end of the world. Ways of becoming a subject and the exercise of the functions that participate in that formation of subjectivity are historical; they constitute the place of power relations between genders. And that model establishes what is to be expected and what is not to be expected in the production of "normal" subjectivities.
>
> (Tort, 2005)

Following that line of thought, we must re-examine our conceptual tools. A spirit open to change is not enough to ensure that, as professionals, we do not form part of the "psychology police", the keeper of the dominant morality, or, almost as bad, operate as politically correct analysts who do nothing to modify their theory to fit their clinical praxis.

And that can easily come to pass if, before the challenges posed by new family forms including those outside heterosexual arrangements or within what is called sexual diversity, we fail to produce the knowledge required to identify and act before the new modalities in which pain and human happiness and unhappiness appear.

To the extent that we undertake the production of that new knowledge, we will realise that our tools and theories are geared towards the malaise and the pathologies of subjects constituted under patriarchy and heteronormativity. And, whether or not we intend to, we often end up upholding the status quo and adapting subjects to the device rather than creating new devices.

The task of producing knowledge is paramount. If we fail to re-examine our conceptual framework, we will end up being the keepers of what was at a certain moment the avant-garde but is today a relic.

To meet the challenges posed by these questions and by the need for specific theoretical innovations, we must not essentialise *historical* modes of the production of desiring subjects, not reify them as transhistorical and invariable.

Regarding the constitution of heterosexual desires today, it is an ethical imperative to understand that what we come upon in patriarchy is not the only possible form of heterosexuality but a particular type of heterosexuality, a heterosexuality that implies the production of desire in relation to unequal difference. Furthermore, we are still in a heteronormative regime, which means that to be heterosexual today is to bear what is seen as a correct or well-adjusted sexuality. It would be very interesting to examine how to develop a heterosexuality outside of inequality, predetermination, and hegemony.

On those ground, our work should revolve around the following:

a   The constitution of heterosexual desire in women in the framework of patriarchal relationships, which implies love for someone who is not only on the other side of sexual difference but also one's social master, someone with privileges that one does not enjoy. As we shall see in Chapter 3, at play in this challenge is the psyche work of being a member of the "devalued gender". More concretely, desiring to belong to the devalued gender requires a specific task for the psyche of women that is not captured on a meta-psychological level by the traditional resolution of the Oedipal complex according to which the major effort in the formation of feminine desire is the abandonment of the first love object—the mother in hegemonic forms of childrearing.

b The constitution of heterosexual desire in men in the framework of patriarchal relationships. At play is a desire that revolves around being the social master. Tendencies that should be analysed not as "natural" but as the historical production of modes of desire include the degradation of masculine erotic life as described by Freud (erotic with the prostitute, tender with the wife) (Freud, 1964 [1910], 12). Silvia Bleichmar shed light on two additional aspects of the constitution of heterosexual masculinity (2005, 2006): the eroticisation of cross-generational relationships between men and masculinisation via the passivization of the older male. Hence, the ethical necessity to reformulate the relationship between the Oedipal complex and the domination-based masculine sexuality through barring adults, mainly men, access to childhood sexuality as way to interdict child sexual abuse.

At stake is ceasing to position Oedipal organisation as inevitable on structural and psychogenetic levels to place it instead in a historical narrative of childrearing in the nuclear family. It must be understood in its real structuring dimension: the triumph of the best of the social over individual egoism insofar as an interdict against the imposition of adult sexuality on children. The Oedipal structure, thus, serves to organise intergenerational relationships and regulate sexuality.

This requires a more complex and non-essentialist understanding of the historical nature of the processes by which desires, heterosexual or diverse, are configured, an understanding tied to childrearing practices. The fact that those processes are historical in no way makes them less real. They may, but do not necessarily, lead to the constitution of new families based on couples (heterosexual or diverse), families with one parent or multiple parents, or other novel formations.

At the same time, we must begin to be able to envision the constitution of desiring modalities outside the hegemonic heteronormative model that has, until recently, been socially necessary to guaranteeing the biological reproduction of the human species.

Relevant here is one of the challenges that queer studies pose to gender studies in the field of subjectivity, mainly ceasing to think of hetero/homoeroticism as discontinuous: The affirmation that sexuation places subjects on one or the other side of these sexual options forever more does not hold up.

At the same time, gender studies must keep reminding queer studies of the central fact that sexed subjectivities are still constituted in the framework of power asymmetries between genders.

In sum, we must be able to grapple simultaneously with how psyches are constituted in relation to:

− The diversity of sexual practices
− The still asymmetrical power relations between genders
− Gender relationships that attempt to elude the patriarchal paradigm

We must do that in order to heed other femininities, masculinities, and diverse sexed identities in formation that are not necessary interested in reproducing patriarchal or heteronormative patterns. Otherwise, we might end up deploying "psychopathology" to send subjects back to the place that they have happily decided to elude.

In the task of altering psychoanalysis to meet contemporary challenges, some problems are more complex than others.

One of the more complex problems is at the core of psychoanalytic theory: the status of sexual difference in the constitution of the psyche. At stake is the notion that the recognition of sexual difference, that is, the representation in the psyche that there are only two positions in desire (feminine and masculine) based on biological differences and that a person can only position himself or herself in one of them. That, for classic psychoanalysis, is what enables the human infant, pursuant to symbolic castration, to gain access to language and the law.

These conceptions still at the core of the psychoanalytic corpus are what prevent the discipline from advancing in, for instance, identifying the realities of children of gay or lesbian couples—their specific psychic experiences seen not in terms of an a priori psychopathologisation of forms of childrearing of couples and parenthoods not organised around that one difference.

Along those lines, we must venture to identify the real clinical problems pertinent to how the meta-psychological is configured in new family formations.

To undertake that necessary task with honesty, we must accept that the toolbox we have to help relieve human suffering was constructed from a heteronormative perspective where sexuality was naturalised and gender essentialised. That means that we know very little about how to diagnose in a way that breaks the ties between the production of subjectivity, on the one hand, and psychopathologies as understood under patriarchy and heteronormativity, on the other. No more is known about how to do so in the field of diverse practices of sexuality and identity or of family models different from the modern nuclear family, particularly in questions of childrearing. That is a crucial part of the challenge we face today.

Other concepts to re-examine are the maternal and paternal functions. The first has been described as the support and protection provided by an adult to enable the sound configuration of the child's psyche, and the second as what enables tolerance of frustration, singularisation, and the ability to confront life's challenges—that is, access to culture and the symbolic order.

Those functions must, of course, be performed by primary caregivers, the ones who accompany a young child through the instances crucial to the constitution of the psyche. But the fact that they are still called maternal and paternal functions and that they are divided by gender reflects the historical construct that is childrearing in a specific framework: modernity's nuclear family.

Many now acknowledge that the biological sex and gender of the one who performs those functions is irrelevant. That said, the continued use of the terms maternal and paternal functions has an often unintentional normalisation effect: it generates an idea/expectation of the "correct" gender of the one who performs each of those functions. Beyond theoretical debates, I am interested in seeing the practical effects of those formulations on clinical devices.

Along these lines, Leticia Glocer (2016) makes a valuable contribution. She observes that when the term "paternal function" is used to refer to breaking up the bond between child and mother insofar as the child is the mother's phallus, a disruption necessary to ushering in culture in a formulation that assigns fatherhood a symbolic function, the mother is located in the terrain of nature and of deficit—that is, in the field of narcissism. There is no recognition, in that classical conception, that the mother can propel separation from the child as a desire of her own. For that and other reasons, Glocer proposes calling that function the third function. She points out that continuing to call it the "paternal function" is a way of universalising what is in fact a symbolic operation tied to a determined society and ideology.

I hold that continuing to use the term "maternal function" to refer to attachment and support operates in an analogous fashion. Another name must be provided, perhaps the frank term "attachment and support function".

And, when they perform those functions, caregivers should be mindful not to appropriate the body of the child as body of boundless pleasure—and that holds true regardless of the gender identity or sexual choice of the adult caregiver in question—since asymmetries of power and knowledge constitute "the very broth in which subjectivity takes shape" (Bleichmar, 2007).

I also believe it is important to stop speaking of the mother in the singular and speak instead of motherhoods in the plural. That is crucial to accompanying women who want or do not want to be mothers at a historical moment when, fortunately, the iron tie between womanhood and the mandate of motherhood is beginning to come undone. In other words, motherhood is no longer always-already conceived as "something" that, on a subliminal level, will supplement the lack of something that a woman will never have. Without that dismantling, we cannot begin to listen to contemporary women and conceptualise that they are not only capable but also desirous of transcendence through their own life and work.

All of that, albeit not without tensions, is at play in the production of what is necessary for the configuration of a child's psyche in childrearing, but never at the price of extra maternal malaise. The formulation is mother *and* child, never mother *or* child, never child to the detriment of the mother.

At the same time, we must heed the fact that women have a spectrum of desires regarding motherhood. Rather than a binary choice of whether to be or not to be a mother, there is an incipient notion of "low-intensity" motherhood. Women, if they are listened to, express that motherhood is, for them, something that may or may not occur in their lives—one desire among many.

Their desire to be mothers depends on the framework in which that motherhood would ensue. In analysis, then, we must interrogate how a woman's reproductive potential is or is not engaged during the period when it exists, understanding it not as fate but as possibility. Analysis is a space to grapple with what place motherhood, as bodily potential, will occupy if chosen.

Similarly, there is a need to reflect on how the stage of maximum professional/intellectual "fertility" coincides with the years of potential biological reproduction. That means that if there is an interest in both a professional life and motherhood, one of the two will not occur at the moment of maximum fertility—and that is something to address for the sake of a conscious choice.

Post-patriarchal, post-heteronormative, and postcolonial psychoanalysis requires that many issues be re-examined from the perspective of contemporary challenges. Motherhood, for instance, must be understood as one desire, alongside desires-related work. At play as well is a willingness to have one's body undergo the changes that gestation brings in what might be an attempt to overcome narcissism and the danger of drowning in self-love.

New Families, New Challenges

Recent years have witnessed new work on childrearing in what are called diverse families.

That began with "assembled families", that is, families constituted after a first or second union that produced offspring on the part of one spouse or both spouses. In Argentina, those situations became more common after divorce and second marriages were legalised in 1987.

Irene Meler (2013) made a major contribution to the psychoanalytic approach to such families from a gender perspective.

Meler discusses the complexities specific to this type of family as well as their diversity, emphasising how these arrangements either favour or aggravate the situation of the women in them. She observes that women often end up taking on far too many responsibilities and men far too few due to how gender relations operate under patriarchy. That is particularly the case after divorce in single-parent homes, where women are often not only the primary caregivers but also the sole economic support. After other relationships are formed, Meler identifies greater hostility on the part of the men in those new relationships towards the children from the prior marriage than on the part of the women in the same situation.

Another aspect characteristic of these assembled families is imposition-transgression or—when exacerbated—authoritarianism-violation as a result of a lack of agreement on what norms should govern the household. In these situations, the man in the new family has the power, supposedly with the woman's consent, but she forges secret and more horizontal alliances against her mate with the children from her first marriage or the children from her current marriage. I have observed what Meler points out in detail in other family models. It is, in practice, a nonconfrontational strategy for women partnered with men whom they consider, either generally speaking or in certain situations, authoritarian or patriarchal. These are strategies to be able to remain in a relationship in the ongoing context of patriarchy as well as attempts not to pass down to the next generation a system in which they no longer believe.

These strategies and the dynamics of imposition and transgression mentioned above can have clinical effects. That said, they must be understood as survival strategies or as scars that patriarchy leaves on the psyche that then operate in heterosexual relationships of domination. They must not be reduced to infringements on a pact of transparency and trust—after all, without parity there can be no genuine pact.

Studies of kinship in these families show that the crisis of blood ties makes way for other alliances and affinities as evident in, for instance, ongoing relationships with members of the former partner's family (ex-mother-, father-, sister-, or brother-in-law). While Meler values ties based on affinity rather than blood, she wonders how durable they are. Will they be abandoned in favour of blood ties in moments of greater need such as old age? Or will genuine solidarity be forged, ties capable of withstanding the need for care at moments of human vulnerability?

She calls attention to another central issue: the tension between children's needs for attachment and stable bonds, on the one hand, and the desires of adults for passionate sexuality and individual success, both of which tend to imperil existing relationships, on the other. That, in my view, is one of the greatest contemporary tensions facing both couples and childrearing.

More recent works address single-parent homes as well as families with diverse configurations as a result of assisted fertility. In the latter case, regardless of the specifics, medical intervention separates conception from the sex act. New practices involving gametes, sperm, or extracted eggs—biological or genetic material donated by third parties—must be studied to shed light on the psyche processes at play in each of those situations or combinations of them, that is, the implications on the psyche of the child and of the adults involved in that intervened gestation.

In my clinical work, which is mainly with adults and adolescents, I have witnessed a number of different situations involving those with the desire to have children. My contact with the effects of these diverse arrangements on the psyche of children, meanwhile, has been through clinical supervision of colleagues who work with them.

In my practice, I have treated heterosexual couples as well as single women and lesbian couples who have had children through the donation of sperm or eggs, as the case may be. I have heard their fantasies about the third parties who provide genetic material, fantasies that range from a sense of otherness to gratitude, to say nothing of fears of having their assets taken away (in these arrangements, like in adoption, more vulnerable sectors tend to donate the genetic material to satisfy more affluent people's desires to become parents).

But that class difference has racial implications as well, since economic inequality disproportionately affects certain racial groups. The parents find themselves raising a child who does not look like them, which can have both internal implications for the subject and entail discrimination at schools pursuant to de facto segregation by class and, by extension, by race in Argentina and elsewhere. International adoptions often bring acute tensions of this sort into families.

At play in each of those desires for parenthood are specific conflicts that must be addressed in clinical practice by sustaining the desire to procreate with whom and how a person chooses, whether or not there is a biological relationship between parent and offspring. That is the foundation for assembling a scene in which to lovingly welcome the child to come into the world, in the case of fertilisation, or into the home, in the case of adoption.

Pertinent here is the work of child psychoanalyst Graciela Woloski (2016). She posits a theory of the configuration of child sexuality in the case of a girl conceived via assisted fertility. Woloski reminds us that beyond how a theory was conceived, its function is always to offer an answer to the mystery of the other's unconscious desire. This girl's parents explained to her, "before you were in mommy's tummy, you were kept warm in a little oven".

I also value her contribution to the analysis of a child raised by a single homosexual male parent (Woloski, 2011). She observes how a fictional life provides the child with refuge and symbolic support to overcome the lack of constant attachment resulting from the separation of the father from his partner, who was the primary caregiver; that care was, after the separation, given by a domestic worker. Woloski addresses all the nuances of the case, specifically: the erotic choice of the parent, that parent's gender position in keeping with the traditional model of masculinity (that is, he was not the site of attachment or support), the mutability of love relationships, and the role of primary caregiver falling on someone hired to do the job after the father's separation. Her work demonstrates a powerful idea I want to convey, mainly the need to grapple with real practices rather than dwell on theoretical speculations.

Another crucial question is the tension between the value of genetics and the will to procreate. Some years ago, I gave a class to colleagues working in the mental health department of the Sociedad de Medicina Reproductiva.[5] They asked me a question specific to the Argentine context: Why do we care so much about genetic analysis in the case of children and grandchildren who, in the context of the military dictatorship (1976–1983), were stolen from their biological parents when, with assisted fertility, we talk about the will procreate as unfettered by genetic possibility?[6] In other words, what really matters? Genetics or childrearing? Together, we decided there is no single answer to that question, and asking it denies the horrific reality that is the theft of children. In the case of children stolen from their parents during the dictatorship, genetics is a tool, not a truth; it is a means to put back together as best possible families that were denied their will to procreate.

Patricia Porchat (2019), meanwhile, discusses how the psychoanalytic device helps "abject"[7] families—that is, families marginalised in society—to become intelligible to the children in them. There is abundant prejudice against those families, and their children are often sent off to "psych" devices by schools, doctors, and social workers. No less important is helping the adults who decide to form these families to be able to resist the dominant norms—and that takes cultural preparation. For that reason and others, many members of diverse families seek therapies that have a gender perspective—and they are right to do so, regardless of what so many of my fellow analysts might think.

Porchat also reflects on the need for the adults in non-traditional families to put together a narrative for their families—a logical precursor (a prequel if you will) for the family stories their children will build. Such narratives are, as Freud pointed out (1964)-1908), a device that enables detachment from family authority. The cast of characters in the non-traditional family narrative might include the father, the mother, the progenitor, and the donor, as well as sometimes phantasmagoric ideas related to those figures, all of them crucial to the development of personal and family imagination. Only after that non-traditional family narrative has been constructed and activated through analysis is it possible to confront the previous generation to then separate from it.

A Closing Reflection

Kinship can be understood as the set of practices that establish relationships of various types to navigate the reproduction of life and the demands of ageing. These are the practices that guide the fundamental forms of human dependence—whether or not intergenerational—at play in birth, childrearing, dependence and emotional support, illness, end of life, and grief, among others (Butler, 2004). Like Porchat, I look to Butler here to underscore the need for the care of others central to kinship ties, both for affect and for protection at certain stages (childhood and old age) or in certain situations (illness, disability, vulnerability, and sorrow).

And it is, in my view, paramount that we deploy our most potent knowledge to give words that validate on a subjective level the ways that people today are—that is, the ways that we are—shaping family relationships insofar as means to meet the need for mutual protection in the face of human vulnerability.

Notes

1 Patriarchy describes a system of organisation of power relations between the genders where men have more social power than women and a hierarchy between men of different generations where the dominant figure is the father/patriarch (Connel 1997).

2 The name of the river that divides Argentina from Uruguay is also used to refer to a region that encompasses both countries.
3 In a research project I directed that was published in my book "Heridos corazones…", (Tajer,2009)I surveyed the families of in-patients ages 35–55 at the time of the study (1997–1999). I found that the experience of the nuclear family was, in the case of the working-class patients interviewed, limited to one generation at the most. Despite that, it formed a social ideal against which family practices were measured.
4 Crucially, before love was brought into the picture, marriage as an institution on which to build a legitimate family was guided, but aspirations tied to patrimony, wealth, work, and reproduction.
5 I am grateful to my colleague Silvia Jadur for the invitation.
6 One of the many horrendous practices during the dictatorship was stealing the children of political prisoners and giving them to families, many of them in or close to the military, who wanted children.
7 Looking to Julia Kristeva, Judith Butler uses this term to speak of what is rejected because seen as not human.

References

Bleichmar, S. (2005) *La subjetividad en riesgo*, Editorial Topía
Bleichmar, S. (2006) *Paradojas de la sexualidad masculina*, Editorial Paidós
Bleichmar, S. (2007) *No me hubiera gustado morir en los 90*, Editorial Taurus
Butler, J. (2004) *Undoing Gender*, Routledge
Connell, R.W. (1997) La organización Social de la Masculinidad, en Valdés, Teresa y Olavarría, José (eds.), *Masculinidad/es. Poder y Crisis*, Ediciones de las Mujeres
Freud, S. (1964) Family Romances, In *The Standard Edition of the Complete Psychological Works of Sigmund Freud, Volume IX.* (1909 [1908]), The Hogarth Press
Freud, S. (1964) A Special Type of Choice of Object made by Men (Contributions to the Psychology of Love, I), In *The Standard Edition of the Complete Psychological works of Sigmund Freud, Volume XI.* (1910) The Hogarth Press
Glocer Fiorini, L. (2016) La nostalgia del padre: ¿Función paterna o función tercera? en Alkolombre, P. y Sé Holovko, Candida (eds.), *Parentalidades y género. Su incidencia en la subjetividad*, COWAP, Editorial Letra Viva
Meler, I. (2013) *Recomenzar: amor y poder después del divorcio*, Editorial Paidós
Porchat, P. (2019) Elementos para reflexionar acerca del trabajo psicoanalítico con familias que 'salen del armario', en *Revista Topía*
Tajer, D. (2009) *Heridos corazones. Vulnerabilidad coronaria en varones y mujeres*, Editorial Paidós
Tort, M. (2005) *Fin du dogme paternel*, Flammarion, Aubier
Woloski, G. (2011) Pascual ve muchas películas. Un niño criado en una familia homoparental, en *Revista de la Sociedad Argentina de Psicoanálisis*, N° 15/16
Woloski, G. (2016) El saber sobre el origen. Ayer y hoy, en Alkolombre, Patricia y Sé Holovko, Candida (eds.), *Parentalidades y género. Su incidencia en la subjetividad*, COWAP, Editorial Letra Viva

Chapter 3

Diversity and Gender in Psychoanalytic Theory and Clinical Practice

In this chapter, I will discuss some of the challenges psychoanalysis faces in addressing the afflictions and the pleasures of the population that does not conform to modernity's heteronormative and binary paradigm.

First, though, I will provide an overview of some of the contributions produced at the juncture between psychoanalysis and gender studies. Those contributions provide both an intellectual platform pursuant to the re-examination of some of the patriarchal, heteronormative, and colonial marks at play in classic psychoanalytic theory and practice and a set of tools with which to address a number of the challenges in psychoanalytic practice today, namely:

a Changes in the configuration of femininities and masculinities, in their respective roles and ideals, in the conformations of desire, and in the historically situated conflicts those changes produce.
b Transformations in the power relations between genders in daily life and the new freedoms, as well as new modes of suffering and pleasure, resulting from those transformations.
c The emergence of multiple family structures that question the immediate and necessary connection between forming a stable romantic relationship and becoming a parent. Examples include assembled families, separation during pregnancy, shared custody of small children, single parenthood as a choice, families of same-sex couples, shared parenthood outside of a romantic relationship, families with three parents, co-motherhood, and others.
d The visibilisation of sexual diversities and non-heteronormative practices.
e The visibilisation of diverse gender identities, including transitions between genders (trans femininities and masculinities, gender-fluid and non-binary individuals).
f The new panorama for procreation, thanks to both reproductive technologies (assisted fertilisation, surrogacy, and the donation of eggs, sperm, and embryos, etc.) and decisions regarding reproduction (a longer reproductive life for women, the alternatives of single parenthood and homosexual families). The desire for biological offspring is no longer bound to a heterosexual couple of reproductive age.

DOI: 10.4324/9781003411253-3

Some may try to look the other way, but changes in the daily life and prospects of today's subjects have an impact on clinical practice as new demands and conflicts set in.

There are two caveats to bear in mind in our approaches to the challenges at hand.

First, we must not, because of prejudices or dated conceptions, see the changes identified above as psychopathological per se. Second, we must not give up the power to identify the forms that psychopathology might adopt in these new psychosocial formations.

Identifying these two risks is an ethical imperative essential to furthering what is, in my view, psychoanalysis's basic commitment to society, namely, working with the forms in which human affliction is expressed, that is, putting pain into words.

In sum, the principal challenge is to consider how psyches are constituted in relation to the diversity of sexual and identity practices, on the one hand, and asymmetrical power relations between genders and the tensions that bring, on the other. Both of those issues must be considered simultaneously. To face that challenge, we must deepen a still incipient dialogue between two currents—queer studies and gender studies—each of which is engaged in its own conversation with psychoanalysis.

Those conversations must understand that psychoanalysis has traditionally rested on the idea that a normal and healthy psyche revolves around recognition of sexual difference, which itself is considered constitutionally binary. There are only two categories: the feminine and the masculine. It must also be grasped that that framework cannot harbour the lived experiences of today's patients. We must not conceive diverse forms of psychosexual development as subaltern to "good forms" or as psychopathological manifestations. Their mere existence must not be seen as a total overhaul of sexual difference in the traditional sense, which means accepting that the fact that desire is not organised around sexual difference does not necessarily mean that sexual difference is not recognised or inscribed in the psyche.

Let us go back in time to look at how, 50 years ago, feminist psychoanalysis reformulated psychoanalytic conceptions of femininities:

a   The abandonment of the notion that masochism is the core of femininity (Freud, 1924–1964b) (Deutsch, 1981) in favour of the notion that masochism in women is a common type of erogeneity constituted in the framework of unequal gender relations where men dominate women (Meler, 1996).

b   A re-examination of the idea that women's superego is poorly developed and, for that reason, they have contributed less to culture. That conception was debunked in Carol Gilligan's pioneering work (1993) on the forms of moral reasoning specific to women. Gilligan's work was later systematised by Nora Levinton (2000).

c   A rethinking of penis envy, understood as envy not of a physical attribute (the penis) but of the social place occupied by men in patriarchy as represented by the penis.

d   The change in the conception of feminine hysteria. Once understood as a "normal" form of womanhood, it was later reconsidered as a compromise solution between the narcissism of the female gender and the practices of sexuality under patriarchy. At play in that compromise is the exercise of seduction by women, on the one hand, and inhibition immediately before consummation because, under patriarchy, the heterosexual sex act brings esteem for women thundering down, on the other (Dío Bleichmar, 1985). In other words, seduce but do not consummate as a strategy to protect one's (self) value.

e   A re-examination of the idea of the desire for a child as essential to the constitution of normal adulthood in women. That revision sees, on the one hand, the desire for a child as an imaginary effect of the relationship between motherhood and femininity as constructed historically in modernity (Badinter,1980; Chodorow,1978); on the other, it makes visible the different ways women who are not mothers, whether or not by choice, become adults.

Another aspect of psychoanalysis that has been re-examined from a gender perspective is the absence of an explicit theory of masculinity. Until very recently, psychoanalysis has had theories of the subject, on the one hand, and of "femininity", on the other—an effect of equating the experience of males with the experience of all human beings through the constitution of a universal subject. Anything that lies outside that paradigm—namely, femininity—is considered a mystery or a black continent that requires separate study. A logical outgrowth of that operation is the denial of masculinity as a specific field; it is subsumed under the notion of the subject. A number of contemporary analysts associated with different tendencies have recently begun to make contributions to this previously neglected field.[1]

Despite that absence of an explicit theory, a contemporary reading of a number of Freud's text can form the basis for a Freudian theory of masculinity. I am thinking of, for instance, "The Most Prevalent Form of Degradation in Erotic Life" (Freud, 1912–1964e), which points out the particularities of the eroticism of cis-hetero masculinity in the framework of modern patriarchal relationships of domination. Freud posits two different types of women: "bad women" whom men look to for sexual pleasure and "good women" whom they choose for marriage. Similarly, the work by Totem and Taboo (1913–1964f), which has been reread countless times for its social and political significance vis-à-vis the constitution of group identity, also sheds light on the formation of a fraternity of men in patriarchy. Freud's text speaks of a father who occupies the place of the law to which he himself is not subject and of the effects of the passage from feudal to modern patriarchy. That passage brought an intra-gender democratisation among men: with the fall of the centralised power of the "pater familiae", power came to be distributed among all adult men.

A number of Freud's clinical experiences with male patients originally proposed as examples of a pathological problem can be read as an analysis of how the masculine psyche was constituted at the time. Consider the cases of Little Hans[2] (1964a–1909), the Rat Man[3] (1964c–1909), the Wolf Man (1964g–1918), and Schreber[4] (1964d–1911).

Another contribution on the part of gender studies to psychoanalysis is emphasis on the tie between relationships of domination, on the one hand, and the construction of modes of subjectivation, on the other. Pertinent to Michel Foucault's study of sexuality and its relationship to power (1986) is an under-explored early facet of Freud's work: the notion of power as a psychological problem. Freud locates power asymmetry principally in the relationships between generations, that is, between parents and children (Benjamin, 1988). His major contributions to understanding obedience before the fear of loss of the other's love has not been duly examined in psychoanalytic theorisation of relations of domination other than those between generations, such as between genders and classes. When any such theorisation is performed, the focus is on the similarities between those other power asymmetries and kinship relations rather than on their specificities.

Two authors have managed to avoid falling into that rote theorisation and made significant contributions to a topic fundamental to the challenges outlined here. In Argentina, Gilou García Reinoso (1998) describes the mechanisms at play in love to the master, the clinical effects of that love, and the need for release from that relationship with the other as absolute master. The other contribution is from North American author Jessica Benjamin (1988). She addresses the specificity of the relationship between power and the constitution of the psyche of each gender in the sociohistorical framework of hierarchy and patriarchy starting at the very early stages of psychic development and through its later development in adulthood. In her theorisation, each bond of love characterised by an asymmetrical power relationship is considered in its specificity, including the bonds between generations.

Significant to this conceptualisation of the constitution of the psyche in a context of patriarchal relationships is the fact that much psychoanalytic clinical practice revolves around how to support the constitution of autonomy in women and how to deconstruct hegemony in men (Fernández, 2000). While there are, of course, multiple expressions of these processes, much clinical intervention with male patients is geared to helping them see the need to conceive of women as peers deserving of equal rights and considerations.[5] And at play for many women patients grappling with subjectivities based on unequal difference is the need to "chop off the head of the headless king" (Rosenberg, 1996). In other words, clinical intervention is oriented to allowing women to capture the difference between the internalised image of man as master—a patriarchal illusion—and real men with their contradictions, fears, and conflicts, and for them to be able to draw that difference without denying the reality of masculine subjectivation grounded on membership in a group with more prerogatives than they themselves enjoy.

Early Feminist Hopes for Psychoanalysis

In formulating these dilemmas, we must not let down our epistemological guard. History holds lesson for feminists, particularly regarding certain illusions.[6] When psychoanalysis emerged, early feminists considered it a scientific ally. After all, a new discipline of the mental field that held that excess repression of sexuality was what caused "modern nervousness", mostly in women, would—they believe—defend the rights of women, and it did to a certain extent (Tubert, 2000). That hope of finding in psychoanalysis a steadfast ally was shattered by the discipline's clinical practice with women. Though they were given a space to elaborate their own narratives about their psychosexual lives, analysts instructed them to find a cure in reproduction and in embracing their role in patriarchal society. There is ample evidence of those clinical practices. An anecdote recounted by Marie Langer,[7] one of the founders of the Asociación Psicoanalítica Argentina, is telling. For years, she had treated a woman who struggled to balance her desire to stay married and raised her child and her professional ambitions. A few years after terminating treatment, Langer ran into a male colleague who told her he was now seeing the woman. Langer asked him how she was managing in her struggle to articulate those two vital desires. Her colleague responded that she had worked it through: she had quit her job and was now a full-time homemaker (Volnovich and Werthein, 1989).

As indicated earlier, in the 1970s the tense relationship and mutual distrust between feminism and psychoanalysis eased somewhat. Contemporary debates revolved around a number of different currents: the Anglo-Saxon school which addresses psychoanalysis and gender, the French school which addresses psychoanalysis and sexual difference, and the Spanish spoken school—the one I form part of—that has drawn on both of those schools in its development.

Revisiting the history of psychoanalysis and feminism can shed light on current psychoanalytic approaches to sexual diversity and help prevent psychoanalysis from becoming an apparatus to reproduce the heteronormative bases of patriarchal society.

To that end, we can begin to entertain the idea that our tools and theories are, in many ways, devised to treat the afflictions and pathologies of subjects by ushering them into heteronormativity. That means we might find ourselves in the paradoxical position of upholding as individuals the inclusion of those who reject heteronormativity while, in our clinical practice, advocating for their de facto exclusion (Reitter, 2023).

An Assessment of the Contributions of Psychoanalysis from a Gender Perspective

The most important advance in psychoanalysis from a gender perspective has been theorising how psyches are constituted in relation to the asymmetry of power between genders. We are today faced with a new task: questioning, first, the binary thinking that lingers on in some aspects of our conception of gender (masculine/feminine) and, second, the notion that sexual object choice (homo/heteroerotic) is discontinuous rather than fluid. Clinical practice, which well exceeds the limitations of those categories, calls on us to embrace this theoretical challenge.[8]

To meet that challenge, we must question one of the medullar cores of psychoanalysis, namely how it conceives of sexual difference and its status in the formation of the psyche, which was discussed in Chapter 1. That is, we must expand our vision of the development of sexuation from being limited to the intrapsychic field to including a political dimension (the role of cultural and historical differences in psychic phenomena and their determination). On that basis, we can begin to reconceptualise the metapsychological. This is particularly pertinent, I would argue, to how same-sex parenthood is being read. When same-sex parenthood is engaged from a metapsychological, and not merely phenomenological, perspective, we see that homosexual eroticism neither ignores nor denies sexual difference. It is just that desire is not caused by that difference, which is by no means the same thing. And that means there is no cause for fear regarding sexual difference when a same-sex couple raises children.

When some fellow analysts characterise same-sex parenthood as "[...] a downright delirium that poses a risk to the basic psychic processes that enable the subject to form a representation of their origin, that is, their childhood sexual theories" (Tort, 2005), they refuse, first, to re-examine conceptual tools and, as a result, to engage today's affective ties, their configuration and specific challenges.

I am very interested in Rosi Braidotti's contributions to contemporary psychoanalysis's approach to the novel configurations discussed here (1994). She subscribes to the idea of nomad subjects first theorised by Gilles Deleuze. Braidotti argues that subjects can move back and forth between modes of desire and identity as part of their vital experiences. Her work focuses on subjective responsibility for the often contingent paths of sexuality and identity.

This conceptualisation provides a way out of the binary between hetero- and homoerotic desire as well as a single and immutable position before sexual difference and gender identity. But no less important is that it does so on the basis of a feminist understanding of power relations between genders. Braidotti's critique of some aspects of Deleuze points out that his notion of becoming minority or "becoming woman"—which is not the same thing—as a way to elude the hegemonic operates differently in the case of those who begin as part of a majority or dominant group than of those who begin in a minority or subaltern group. Those in that second group have had to deal with the marks of subordination in the constitution of their psyches. These unequal points of departure imply different processes of transformation in what we now call the subject's deconstruction of the marks of patriarchal hegemony.

Another contribution is the conceptual development of the triad operative in processes of subjectivation: gender, sex, and sexuation. Gender, in the field of social theory, is the cultural and social construction of sex insofar as "a set of contingent signifieds that sexes assume in the context of a given society" (Lamas, 1996). At play in that construction are, among other things, asymmetrical power relations and different roles for those sexes in the framework of patriarchy. Regarding gender subjectivation, some assert that identity and processes of identification are at its core.[9] Others hold that elements such as the object of drives, the formation of ideals, and modes of narcissism are key to gender subjectivation.[10]

Sex, meanwhile, refers to the biological order with its specificities and differences. But the idea of biological sex is complicated by at least three factors. First, the very notion of the biological as an immutable order is now in crisis, thanks to gender-affirming surgery, reproductive technologies, hormone therapy, implants, the removal of sex traits, etc. Second, the existence of intersex subjects casts doubt on the idea that humanity in its entirety can be divided into two biological categories: the male and the female. Third, sex and biology are signified from the outset; that is, there is no "natural" approach to biology. It is always filtered through some sort of pattern of signification (Butler, 1993).

Finally, within the topic of sexuation, there are also at least two currents of thought: (a) those who consider sexuation the very foundation of the psychoanalytic field. At play in sexuation, they argue, is the drive that inhabits and determines the space of psychic reality, that is, the unconscious subjective dimension that grows out of the symbolic sexual difference in which any speaking subject is constituted; this reality should not be confused with biological or social reality; and (b) those who hold that gender is also a psychoanalytic category and see sexuation as constituted in the broader processes of subjectivation in which, in turn, the historical and social framework plays a part.

Some of the thinking of feminists who form part of the Lacanian school falls into that first category. And here, in my view, lies one of the problems that require further elaboration and debate. To grapple with the challenges that sexual and identity diversities present to psychoanalysis, we must avoid being restricted by stiff concepts developed in a heteronormative framework. As stated, some theories helpful to grappling with cis-heterosexual practices can be obstacles to a non-pathologising conceptualisation of the diverse. How to envision practices that exceed the "normativised"? And how to grapple with the new practices and modes of desire that take shape as the world ceases to be so very binary in its formulation of gender identity and its acquisition, and so very heteronormative in its formulation of the erogenous?

Beyond the differences identified here, psychoanalysts who engage feminism agree that none of these factors can be considered in isolation or as capable in and of itself of grasping what determines the dynamic relationships between genders and modes of subjectivation.

If these various factors are isolated rather than articulated, there is a risk of reductionism, which often takes one of the following forms:

- Sociologism, that is, the attempt to explain sexuation entirely through the assumption of social roles;
- Biologism, that is, the naturalisation, medicalisation, and behaviourist sexologisation of the sexual without regard for the unconscious dimension of desire;
- Psychologism, that is, a vision of the symbolic system that upholds and determines sexed places as an ahistorical structure, and male domination as an invariable and necessary expression of that structure (Rosenberg, 1996).

After these reflections, we will see how the tools constructed by a gender perspective on psychoanalysis provide us with a sound basis from which to confront the current challenges posed by the diverse practices of those who come to us for treatment.

Perversion?

Hard though it is to believe, there are still some analysts who define perversion as any sexual practice at odds with dominant morality. In other words, perversion is still, though not necessarily explicitly, identified with non-hegemonic sexual practises and non-heterosexual practices.[11] A single course for the development of sexual difference and its relationship to symbolic castration is upheld in relation to the constitution of the psyche. That perspective necessarily sees anything "new" as pathological and, hence, fails to grasp what might actually be pathological in the new.

My understanding of perversity is different insofar as it rests on the status in one´s psyche of the person with whom a given sexual practice is performed, not the practice in and of itself (Bleichmar, 2005). Regardless of whether the practice is hetero or homo, whether it takes place in the context of a couple or a threesome or anything else, the pertinent question is whether the other person or persons are objectified or seen as peers deserving of the same consideration and ethical treatment as oneself. The answer to those questions, not the practice, is what determines the position of the subject as well as the presence or absence of perversion. This approach heeds the metapsychology rather than the phenomenology at play in a given situation.

The Desire of having a Child by a Same-Sex Couple people

Same-sex parenthood is now not only a topic of debate but also a reality. In Argentina, it has been protected and legitimised since 2010 by the Marriage Equality Act, which has effects on the field of psychology, among others. Among my fellow psychoanalysts, some are worried about how being raised by a same-sex couple will affect children. Will these children be afflicted by mental illness because conceived and raised by a couple that "rejects sexual difference"? Others fear that a greater proportion of these children will be homosexual than those born to heterosexual couples. That, in my view, is entirely possible: the demise of the heteronormative mandates may well open up a wider panorama of sexual diversity. But is that a problem? And if so, for whom? In any case, scientific data collected thus far shows no greater rate of sexually diverse children raised by same-sex parents than by their heterosexual counterparts (Patterson, 2014). Some colleagues speak of the "lesser evil" of adoption of older kids by same-sex couples because it is "better than being brought up in an orphanage".

The universe of same-sex parenthood is very diverse, ranging from children born to heterosexual couples who now live with one of their parents (usually the mother) and their same-sex partner to children born to same-sex couples through assisted fertility, surrogacy, or adoption. A variety of situations often surface together, even though they are not all limited to same-sex parents. The children in the first case, that is, those born to heterosexual couples but now living in a same-sex household, have also been through a divorce or a parental death, which means they are also children of assembled families. Children born through assisted fertility have their own set of issues regardless of the sexual orientation of those who raise them (Ormart, 2018). And surrogacy, which is highly regulated in Argentina and hence mostly performed abroad, requires money and foreign travel. With surrogacy, the child is conceived and born in another country. For all these reasons, this option is available only to a small number of people. Similarly, with adoption the complexity of the situation far exceeds the sexual orientation of the persons who adopt.

Let us take a look at how these topics have been dealt with in the psychoanalytic milieu and discuss some of the concerns fellow psychoanalysts have expressed, concerns that vary if the couple in question consists of two women or of two men. I hope that a post-patriarchal, post-heteronormative, and postcolonial perspective will be able to open our ears and expand the range of interventions we undertake in psychoanalysis.

- **Lesbian motherhoods:** I have been struck by an odd articulation (Torres Arias, 2005): some analysts of the French school of psychoanalysis defends diversity and the right of lesbian couples to raise children. At the same time, it insists on the need for those couples to find a significant male figure to effect the rupture in the mother-child dyad, that is, in my view, a high price to pay at the altar of dogma. If we hold that the father figure who breaks up that dyad is a historic construct at the service of traditional forms of male domination to assure fathers a monopoly on the symbolic function, then accepting lesbian motherhoods but at the same time arguing for the need for that rupturing masculine presence/function seems like an unnecessary burden. That insistence serves, it would seem, to continue to uphold the dogma that there is only one possible symbolic order and only one means of access to it. As explained in Chapter 2, one of our tasks as analysts is to support the organisation of what we might call a minority family narrative that can later help the child to construct their own primary scene. Once again, the idea is not to see lesbian motherhoods as lesser than "normal" or desirable heterosexual parenthood but to grapple with them in their specificities.

- **Gay fatherhoods:** The idea of homosexuality as perverse by definition is particularly acute in the case of gay men. At the same time, there is a widespread notion that men, regardless of sexual orientation, should not touch the body of babies or young children because male sexuality is seen as unstoppable and unethical; those bodies will be violated and perverted if men are its primary caregivers (Volnovich, 2000). Indeed, Volnovich argues that, in order to generate new practices of fatherhood, men, like women historically, must be careful not to impose adult sexuality on children's bodies. He argues that if that line is crossed, the child's psyche will be caught up in an unmanageable trauma (Bleichmar, 2005). That widespread fear of how children will be affected when adult men are their primary caregivers is heightened when those men are homosexual. That prejudice must be combated in any effort to understand and accept new family configurations. At stake here—and, indeed, throughout this book— is differentiating between pathology, prejudice, and resistance. Patterson's research in the United States (2014) supports what clinical practice suggests: most childhood sexual abuse within families is at the hands of adult heterosexual men and aimed at girls; homosexual men are not, then, the ones who pose the greatest risk.

Furthermore, there are now years of experience with gay male fatherhood (single parents, gay couples, or three-way parenting arrangements). The pressing task today is less to combat prejudice than to support narratives of these experiences, their specificities and the challenges they present for psychoanalytic practice.[12]

The Desire to Have a Child Alone

- **Single women who want to have children:** There is nothing new about women raising children on their own, but on the level of the imaginary that was always seen as a terrible fate or the result of abandonment on the part of the father. Now, however, it is a choice, albeit one that is met with immense criticism and disdain: that degree of autonomy in women is unbearable in a patriarchal framework and mistaken for narcissism. Indeed, the act of autonomy of a woman deciding to have a child on her own must be read in relation to an enduring central tenet of male power over women: the refusal to "give a child" to a woman during the period of a woman's life when she can conceive through sex. Given that male reproductive capacity lasts far longer than female reproductive capacity, women today are more and more inclined to separate the decision to have a child from the decision to have a life partner.[13] Women thus escape the trap and submission implied by any delay in that decision on the part of a male partner. Significantly, one of my first lessons in the field of psychoanalysis from a gender perspective was that women in stable heterosexual relationship can also fall into narcissism when they reduce the male with whom they have a child to a mere inseminator and provider instead of considering him as a real partner. I also learnt, in my clinical practice, that one might sympathise personally and politically with the idea of a woman deciding to have a child on her own, while, as a psychoanalyst, sometimes we identify cases of women who have trouble even taking care of themselves; cases were the need to care for an other can throw off their delicate psychic balance. This places an ethical responsibility on us to identify the different layers of each particular situation.

• **Single men who want to have children:** This is nothing new either: men of different sexual orientations have wanted to have children on their own, regardless of who bears it. What is new is the open expression of that desire and the possibilities opened up by reproductive technologies, by women willing to co-parent outside of a romantic relationship or to offer their uteruses in surrogacy arrangements. (As mentioned above, the high cost of surrogacy and the regulations limiting it in Argentina have had the effect of pushing those practices and arrangements abroad; surrogacy is, as a result, an option for a select group of very wealthy men). To assess the impact of father-only households on children and modes of childrearing, we will have to observe these practices over time.[14] The most common option for single men who want to raise children is adoption of older children or teenagers or the provision of foster care, which necessarily entails shared parenting. Experiences of male foster parents appear to be largely positive. The most common practice of all is single men who begin to act as primary caregivers after the break-up of a family or the death of their partner and co-parent.

Trans and Intersex People

In their own words, trans people are those whose identities and lifestyles have shifted from the gender they were assigned at birth on the basis of their biological traits. The diagnosis in the DSM,[15] a reference manual for psychiatry in the United States, is gender dysphoria. That diagnosis authorises gender reassignment that often includes surgery and hormone therapy. When backed by a mental health professional, it also enables the person in question to change their legal identity to reflect their experience of their gender. That criterion was adopted as the model in Argentina until the Gender Identity Act of 2012. In Argentina, that law falls within the realm of the right to identity,[16] not the realm of psychopathology as it does in many other regions, which opens up a wide range of possibilities discussed in Chapter 4.

The Argentine law allows anyone who requests a change in gender identity to make that change in their government-issued documents. It also ensures access to hormone treatment and gender-affirming surgery at the healthcare system (public or private) if requested (surgery is not required to gain access to the right to change identity). This law reflects the range of trans identities, from those who want to have gender-affirming surgery to those who receive hormone treatment and those who change their gender identity without changing their original genitalia. A gain made in the past decade is that it is no longer required to change gender within the male/female binary: trans masculinity and trans femininity are now legally recognised options. Indeed, it is now possible in Argentina to have a non-binary identity on government-issued documents without any prior legal requirements.[17] The law also requires that in educational, health care, and work environments a person be called by the name and gender they perceive as their own, regardless of what their government-issued documents may say. This is a major advance with significant effects for the subjectivation and rights of all gender configurations.

Regardless of all those who claim that the question of identity is passé and ultimately an illusion, we see that in the same historical moment two polar positions coexisting: there are those who are willing to operate on their erogenous organs so that their genitals "match" their gender identity, and there are those who oppose those operations because they deem them a price too high to pay for normativisation. Those in that second group claim the right to live and be recognised as the sex and gender they experience without operations.

While any decision about one's own body deserves respect, gender-affirming surgery is potentially, among other things, a mode to discipline bodies by adapting them to hegemonic norms. In many cases, the body loses the ability to have orgasms since sex organs are replaced by a cavity or prothesis, as the case may be. There is now extensive experience with people who are satisfied with their gender-affirming surgery—or surgeries, since often more than one operation is required. Others are not satisfied, their ideals unmet by the operations. It is important, therefore, to accompany each person's decisions and help them to clarify their expectations and hopes regarding each step they take towards aligning their sex and their gender.

The term "intersex" refers to persons with ambiguous sex traits or with XXY or XO genes. Intersex activists support the position taken by the parents in the film *XXY*: They decided not to operate on their intersex child when that child was a baby. In the film, the teenage protagonist assumes a female gender identity. Her sex drive is tied to her masculine genitalia, and her object choice heterosexual in terms of gender identity but homosexual in terms of genitalia. As the film indicates, we are witnessing a moment when categories explode; we appear to be near what Paul B. Preciado (2003) describes as "multitudes queer".

That reflection in no way invalidates those who opt for gender-affirming surgery to adjust their body to match their identity. It is fundamental that medical intervention not be premature; the person in question must make the decision when they decide to. An operation is not the same thing as a name change, in part because the former is irreversible. We will discuss this further in Chapter 4.

The framework for any discussion, though, is the multiplicity of positions subjects assume in their own experiences of the relationship between sex, gender, and sexuation.

In sum, we must be careful to keep a discipline or field like psychoanalysis from attempting to rebind sexuality and biology in a repetition of some of psychiatry's most homophobic practices (Sanz, 2004). Psychoanalysis was a pioneer in uncoupling psychosexuality and biology. We must look to that tradition to avoid unwittingly being party to conservative strains of thought and practice that psychopathologise any sexuality that differs from the heteronormative. Similarly, we can find ourselves participating in groups that advocate "curing" homosexuality, bisexuality, transsexuality, transgenderism, and transvestitism.

The most honest position may well be to admit that the clinical and theoretical tools we have are designed to relieve human suffering, but from a heteronormative perspective where sex is naturalised and gender essentialised. We are learning how to diagnose such that the production of subjectivity and historical sexuation is released from the tethers of psychopathologies in our approach to sexual and identity diversity—one of the key challenges facing us today.

Notes

1 Michel Tort, Silvia Tubert, Sergio Rodriguez- Ricardo Estacolchic, Ernesto Sinatra, Silvia Bleichmar, Juan Carlos Volnovich, Mabel Burin, Irene Meler, and Facundo Blestcher, to name a few.
2 Analysis of phobia in a five-year-old boy.
3 A case of obsessive neurosis.
4 Note on a case of paranoid described in the first person.
5 For greater analysis of how this operates in clinical practice and in life, see Chapter 5.
6 We will return to this topic in Chapter 9.
7 A pioneering thinker on these issues, her book *Maternidad y Sexo. Estudio psico-analítico y psicosomático* [*Motherhood and Sexuality*], first published in 1951, has been translated into a number of languages; there have been over 40 re-editions in

Spanish. English Version Motherhood and Sexuality. The Guilford Press, 1992, tanslated by Nancy Caro Hollander

8 In my clinical practice, I have often accompanied patients as they form sexual and affective ties with persons of both sexes without feeling the need to embrace a specific identity. Regarding identity, there are, of course, people who consider themselves non-binary, trans male, trans female, and so on. See Chapter 6.

9 See Chapter 4.

10 As developed in Chapter 1.

11 Perversion is read as denial of the "no" that channels desire towards someone on the other side of "sexual difference". Even when accompanied by a claim not to level moral judgements, this pronouncement of perversion without any attempt at explanation is a "diagnostic insult" (Ayouch, 2015).

12 Along these lines, see Chapter 2.

13 That is even the case if a woman is in a relationship with someone who does not want to have children. Today, women can have children on their own while remaining in a relationship with someone who will not be a co-parent.

14 One paradigmatic case that was covered widely in the media involved a 40-year-old man from the province of Córdoba, Argentina, who had lived in Spain for years. He published an ad on the Internet saying he was looking for a surrogacy arrangement with an Argentine woman. A woman who was younger and poorer than the man expressed interest, and he chose her. When the two met in person, they "fell in love" and decided to have the child together. Two years later, they split up. She was undocumented in Spain; he argued that she was a "bad mother" because immature; he claimed she lacked the economic and legal resources to raise the child. He went to court to get sole custody. A first reflection is that we should believe someone when they say they want to raise a child on their own. Denying that to uphold the value of romantic love prevents us from seeing the effects that often passing impulses might eventually have. Once again, the relationship between body, power, reproductive capacity, class, immigration status, and risk is brought to the surface.

15 Now in its fifth edition, the *Diagnostic and Statistical Manual of Mental Disorders*, known as the DSM (American Psychiatric Association (2013), is a handbook put together by the American Psychiatric Association [sic] and used internationally to classify "disorders" and mental health problems. It contains a chapter, CIE-10, written by international experts at the World Health Organisation.

16 This area of the law and of human rights is quite developed in Argentina because of the large number of children of individuals disappeared by the state during the dictatorship (1976–1983) who were illegally appropriated by military families and others with ties to the military. I explore this question in greater depth in Chapter 4.

17 Since 2022.

References

American Psychiatric Association (2013) *Diagnostic and Statistical Manual of Mental Disorders Fifth Edition DSM-5*, APA

Ayouch, T. (2015) *Géneros, Cuerpos y Placeres. Perversiones psicoanáliticas con Michel Foucault*, Editorial Letra viva

Badinter, E. (1980). *L'amour en plus. Histoire de l'amour maternel*, Flammarion

Benjamin, J. (1988) *The Bonds of Love. Psychoanalysis Feminism and the Problem of Dominication*, Pantheon

Bleichmar, S. (2005) *La subjetividad en riesgo*, Editorial Topía

Braidotti, R. (1994) *Nomadic Subjects: Embodiment and Sexual Difference in Contemporary Feminist Theory*, Columbia University Press

Butler, J. (1993) *Bodies that Matter. On the Discursive Limits of "Sex"*, Routledge

Chodorow, N. (1978) *The Reproduction of Mothering: Psychoanalysis and the Sociology of Gender*, The Regents of the University of California

Deutsch, H. (1981) La importancia del masoquismo en la vida mental de la mujer, en Fliess, R. (comp.), *Escritos psicoanalíticos fundamentales*, Editorial Paidós

Dio Bleichmar, E. (1985) *El feminismo espontáneo de la histeria. Estudio de los trastornos narcisistas de la femineidad*, Adotraf

Fernández, A.M. (2000) Autonomías y de-construcciones de poder, en Meler, Irene y Tajer, Débora (comps.), *Psicoanálisis y Género. Debates en el Foro*, Lugar Editorial

Foucault, M. (1986) *The History of Sexuality 3. The Care of the Self*, Pantheon Books

Freud, S. (1964a) Analysis of a Phobia in a Five-Year-Old Boy, In *The Standard Edition of the Complete Psychological Works of Sigmund Freud, Volume X*. (1909) The Hogarth Press

Freud, S. (1964b) The Economic Problem of Masochism, In *The Standard Edition of the Complete Psychological Works of Sigmund Freud, Volume XIX*. (1924) The Hogarth Press

Freud, S. (1964c) Notes Upon a Case of Obsessional Neurosis, In *The Standard Edition of the Complete Psychological Works of Sigmund Freud, Volume X*. (1909) The Hogarth Press

Freud, S. (1964d) Psycho-Analytic Notes on an Autobiographical Account of a Case of Paranoia (Dementia Paranoides), In *The Standard Edition of the Complete Psychological Works of Sigmund Freud, Volume XII*. (1911) The Hogarth Press

Freud, S. (1964e) A Special Type of Choice of Object made by Men (Contributions to the Psychology of Love, I), In *The Standard Edition of the Complete Psychological works of Sigmund Freud, Volume XI*. (1910) The Hogarth Press

Freud, S. (1964f) Totem and Taboo, In *The Standard Edition of the Complete Psychological Works of Sigmund Freud, Volume XIII*. (1913 [1912–1913]) The Hogarth Press

Freud, S. (1964g), From the Historiy of an Infantile Neurosis, in *The Standard Edition of the Complete Psychological works of Sigmund Freud, Volume XVII*. (1918 [1914]) London: The Hogarth Press

García Reinoso, G. (1998) Reconocimiento del otro y de la articulación con el otro, para amar en el amor y en la amistad en *Revista Postdata*, N° 2

Gilligan, C. (1993) *In a Different Voice*, Harvard University Press

Lamas, M. (1996) Usos, dificultades y posibilidades de la categoría 'género', en Lamas, Marta (comp.), *El género: la construcción cultural de la diferencia sexual*, Editorial Porrúa

Langer, M. (1951) *Maternidad y sexo. Estudio psicoanalítico y psicosomático*, Paidós

Levinton Dolman, N. (2000) *El superyó femenino. La moral en las mujeres*, Biblioteca Nueva

Meler, I. (1996) Psicoanálisis y género. Aportes para una psicopatología, en Burin, Mabel y Dio Bleichmar, Emilce (comps.), *Género, psicoanálisis, subjetividad*, Editorial Paidós

Ormart, E. (comp.) (2018) *Cuerpos y familias transformados por las técnicas de reproducción asistida*, Editorial Letra Viva

Patterson, C. (2014) Madres lesbianas, padres gays y sus hijos e hijas: una síntesis de resultados de investigación, en *Revista Topía*

Preciado, P.B. (2003) Multitudes queer. Notas para una política de los "anormales". Multitudes. *Revue politique, artistique, philosophique, 12*. vol. 2, 17–25

Reitter, J. (2023) *Heteronormativity and Psychoanalysis, Oedipus Gay*, Routledge

Rosenberg, M. (1996) Género y sujeto de la diferencia sexual. El fantasma del feminismo, en Burín, Mabel y Dio Bleichmar, Emilce (comps.), *Género, Psicoanálisis y Subjetividad*, Editorial Paidós

Sanz, J. (2004) *Teoría queer y psicoanálisis*, Síntesis

Tort, M. (2005) *Fin du dogme paternel*, Flammarion, Aubier

Torres Arias, M.A. (2005) Reflexiones psicoanalíticas sobre maternidad y paternidad en parejas homosexuales, en *Debate Feminista*, Año 16, Vol. 32

Tubert, S. (2000) Sobre la moral sexual. Psicoanálisis y feminismo, en Meler, I. y Tajer, D. (comps.), *Psicoanálisis y Género. Debates en el Foro*, Lugar Editorial

Volnovich, J.C. y Werthein, S. (comps.) (1989) *Marie Langer. Mujer, Psicoanálisis y Marxismo*, Contrapunto

Volnovich, J.C. (2000) Generar un hijo: la construcción del padre, en Meler, Irene y Tajer, Débora (comps.), *Psicoanálisis y Género. Debates en el Foro*, Lugar Editorial

Chapter 4

Trans Childhoods as Possible Childhoods

It is imperative that psychoanalysis from a gender perspective grapple with trans childhoods. In so doing, we must not fall into the temptation to devise a "special" psychoanalysis for "special" populations, but rather shape a psychoanalysis that has room for everyone.

Trans children are children who from a very young age manifest "nonconformity" between the gender they were assigned at birth on the basis of their biological sex traits and their gender identity on the basis of how they perceived themselves.

The ethical thinking and commitment develop here is located: its framework is how, in the south of this planet, the imaginaries and practices of subjects are changing regarding their vital bonds. Those changes in imaginaries and subjects are accompanied by legislation that sanctions them. I am referring specifically, in the Argentine case, to gender-identity laws[1] and the Marriage Equality Act[2] passed in recent years.

I will relate this change in collective imaginaries with individual yearnings and life projects, in this case during childhood. Like the horizon, those yearnings and projects change as we advance toward them. I will also venture to understand trans childhood from the perspective of a contemporary psychoanalysis up to today's challenges.

My approach to trans childhood bears in mind three interrelated issues part and parcel of these times in Argentina:

1 Advances in the legal framework in the sphere of gender and the expansion of rights
2 New ways of being and desiring
3 New clinical challenges resulting from these advances

1 Advances in Legal Frameworks

The law governing gender identity in Argentina is extremely progressive. It postulates that to change one's identity so that it matches one's self-perception is a right. The framework for that law is the broader right to identity, a highly

DOI: 10.4324/9781003411253-4

developed area in Argentina tied to human rights. In Argentina, a legal change in identity requires neither the authorisation of a psychiatrist or a psychologist nor a surgical intervention as it does in other countries, where "transgenderism" is considered a psychopathology.

In many countries, a diagnosis from a mental-health specialist is required before someone with "that problem" is authorised to change identity; in some countries, gender-affirming surgery is even required. The spirit of Argentina's law on gender identity, like its law on mental health,[3] is entirely different. Both were enacted during the same period. Both are heirs to the right to identity laws passed in Argentina, thanks to the efforts of human rights organisations to restore the identity of children kidnapped from political prisoners disappeared during the last dictatorship in Argentina (1976–1983).

The situation of trans rights in Argentina is different from, for example, the United States or France. Other imaginaries are at play around human rights in general and the right to identity from a young age in particular, and that is both reflected in and produced by a legal framework that differs from ones where a change in gender identity is only possible pursuant to a psychiatric diagnosis or, in some cases, even a surgical intervention.

2   New Modes of Being and Desiring

The emergence of trans childhoods that must be heeded from a young age is associated, in my view, with a new framework of social practices and legal recognition. That framework is crucial to letting those childhoods come to light and, hopefully, receive caring acceptance from the families and therapists of trans children. This connection between the law and imaginaries informed decades-long work (Fernández and Tajer, 2006) on clandestine abortion and feelings of guilt, and how the legalisation of abortion in Argentina has alleviated those feelings (Tajer, 2019).

To illuminate that connection, I look to what queer studies have contributed to clinical psychology regarding the suffering that comes with living in the "closet".[4]

The closet in this metaphorical sense is a powerful device to regulate dissident sexualities and bodies (Sedgwick,1990). Practices, identities, and love outside the heteronormative or binary paradigm cannot live under the light of day; they are relegated to the confines of bathrooms, bedrooms, and only certain city neighbourhoods. A biopolitical device, the closet as a component of subjectivation processes generates angst, depression, and anxiety.

Colleagues have asked me—or told me they have asked themselves—about cases like Lulú's,[5] the one that gave rise to the reflections offered in the chapter. They wonder if Lulú isn't too young to change identity. Isn't it harmful, they ask, to "close" at such a young age something that should remain "open"?

To them I respond that these are the challenges posed to clinical practice in this new post-closet phase of history. I understand that what happens to certain children at a younger age today than at other historical moments has to do with the removal of the inhibitions and domestications enacted by the closet on subjects who wanted to avoid additional suffering from incomprehension and discrimination. The earlier emergence of dissident sexualities or identities might also be because there are now words to signify that early experience, words understood by the ones having those experiences and by those close to them.

At the same time, taking on a new identity does not bring any process to a close. It is—or is not—a necessary step in a transition that does not have a predetermined end. When that step is both necessary and taken, it usually has a positive impact on subjects' in terms of ownership and mental health.

I would like to present here as well the flipside of openness to trans child-hoods. Lohana Berkins's[6] account of her childhood as a trans girl. When she was a child, her family "tolerated" that she wanted to wear girls' clothes, thinking that it was "just a passing phase". That attitude afforded a peaceful childhood, at least in that respect. But as the teenage years set in, that tolerance became fierce intolerance. She had to leave her middle-class home in a small town in Argentina at the age of 13.[7] She moved to the capital of her province where she worked as a prostitute to survive.

On the basis of that case and others, I conclude that what is tolerated but not accepted or recognised will sooner or later cease to be tolerated and be met with cruelty, or even banishment. "Tolerance" actually hides the hope that "that thing" will disappear in adolescence or adulthood, and brutality[8] appears before its persistence.

Not all trans children, however, feel the need, as Lulú did, to request a change in identity on their government-issued documents. Many just ask to be accepted, to be recognised in a manner in keeping with how they perceive themselves, and to be called by the names they choose for themselves and the corresponding pronouns. No more and no less. They simply ask to be recognised as themselves.

Relevant here is one of the findings of research performed on childhood, health, and gender (Tajer et al., 2015). Professionals from different areas of children's health agree that the suffering experienced by trans and sexually diverse children is tied not to psychopathology but to discrimination.[9] A later study that also dealt with a trans and sexually diverse population, this time in adolescence, found that the group of mental-health professionals interviewed considered "transgenderism", but not sexual diversity, a psychopathology. This suggests that the spheres of health and mental health no longer psycho-pathologies a priori sexual diversity and that they are accepting of flexibility in children's game and roles; they do not subscribe to the strict stereotypes of pink for girls and blue for boys. There is, nonetheless, insistence on moni-toring future development. Sometimes that is a necessary precaution, but sometimes what is at play is a sense of askance, especially when early in life a diverse identity or expression of gender sets in. It appears that gender diversity is harder to accept amongst those who work with adolescents. The dynamic may be similar to what we saw with Lohana; that is, the flipside of tolerance in childhood is rejection in adolescence because tolerance is not the same thing as loving acceptance.

The fact that a psychic apparatus has settled into a gender identity that differs from a biological sex is, it seems, still unsettling (Paván, 2016).

3 New Clinical Challenges

For the post-patriarchal and post-heteronormative clinical practice I am attempting to systematise in this book, there is a need to break the bonds between what are historical modes of identity and what is called "normal" psychosexuality in order to grapple with the fact that (much of) "today's psychopathology is tomorrow's (psycho) sexuality" (Barzani, 2015).

After that is established, from what place and with what tools can we intervene on the psychoanalytic field? To be able to more lovingly accept those experiencing trans childhoods, we must delve further into new clinical challenges.

Clinical work with trans children must heed the rights of those children and engage in post-patriarchal and post-heteronormative listening. Special care must be taken not to slip into, no matter how unwittingly, the idea that what takes place in the office of the mental-health professional has nothing to do with the surrounding legal framework or into what we might call a "desiring spiritualism" where a subject has no body or history. The notion of "desiring spiritualism" was developed by Silvia Bleichmar as a critique of the ahistorical nature of much psychoanalysis that envisions the subject as a psyche apparatus in itself. No mind is paid to the interrelationship between that psyche and the material conditions in which it exists, among them the vicissitudes of the body and the social imaginaries at play in each historical moment and cultural space. All of that is reduced to the background where the subject's own psychic drama unfolds. That latter risk appears when intrapsychic determinations are considered the only one worth, with an exclusion of all others determinations in the constitution of the psyche. Added ti the consideration of the insertion of the child into one and only one, by definition universal,[10] legitimate symbolic order.[11] The primary determinant in the constitution of the psyche is, from that classic perspective, the parents' desire for the subject in formation. And those parental desires are seen as basically derived from parents' phantasmatic; in the case of trans children, this perspective holds that the parents'—usually the mother's—pathogenic desire for a daughter rather than a son or vice versa is responsible for the trans child. What is ignore, or even invisibilised, in that conception is that the mother is in fact a speaking subject. And as a speaking being, she is not only the bearer of imaginary meanings specific to a given society but also the spokesperson of thousands of past generations (Castoriadis, 1975)—and that holds true for the formation of all identities, not only ones that "deviate from the norm".

Post-patriarchal psychoanalysis locates parents' desires in the constitution of the psyche and gender identity of the trans child in a socio-historical framework, one that, in the Argentine cases, is characterised by:

- A law on gender identity inscribed in the legal framework of the broader right to identity. In this post-closet period, that legal framework enables parents to identify, understand, and support the early expressions of their trans children.
- The resulting demand on the part of even young trans children to be recognised according to their gender identity, which is often eventually accepted by at least one of their parents or guardians.
- Parents who are willing to let identities flow more freely, without the need to quickly encapsulate into categories represented by, for instance, pink for girls and blue for boys.
- Challenges regarding how psychoanalytic theory and the "psychoanalytic ear" deal with all this.

How would a psychoanalysis that locates the patient in a socio-historical framework operate around issues of sexual and gender diversity? It would, among other things, hold that sexuality always and for all subjects disrupts nominal categories; it would uphold the unconscious dimension of sexuation. And that would explain, for instance, how a mother[12] who states that she does not believe she desired that her biologically male child be biologically female speaks from the field of the conscious, which is not the only field that determines sexuation—the unconscious operates in that determination as well. So far, so good—no dispute between the perspective of classic psychoanalysis and psychoanalysis from a gender perspective. The disputes begin when, on that basis, it is argued that the question of rights is minor. Adopting a new gender, social, and legal identity—this line of reason goes—would in no way alleviate the suffering of a trans girl, say, because for her—like for all speaking beings—sexuality exceeds language categories.

It is easy to argue that nothing would change in the slightest if you are a cis person who enjoys, and has always enjoyed, the rights and privileges that come with that. Things are quite different if you are not. That supposed sameness ("nothing would change in the slightest") dismisses real lived difference and its effects on subjects.

Another difference in the conception of post-patriarchal and classic psychoanalysis is that an early truth—a trans identity from a young age, say—is necessarily innate, which would mean that gender is innate. But if, as I argue, it is not innate, that does not mean it is the result of a "maternal ravage". What is unthinkable in a psychoanalysis that has not problematised the marks of patriarchy it bears is that a child early on assumes their own gender-diverse identity.

Furthermore, even if we agree that sexuation, for post-patriarchal psychoanalysis, is in its origins external to the subject, here we are talking about identity, not sexuation. From the perspective of feminist psychoanalysis, there is no correspondence between biological sex, gender identity, object choice, and sexed position. Multiple combinations of those dimensions are not only possible, but actual.

Childhood and Gender Identity

How, then, does gender identity take shape?

Emilce Dio Bleichmar (1996), who traced the history of our understanding of the relationship between gender identity and the constitution of the psyche, found that John Money was responsible for bringing the term "gender", which comes from the science of language, to the life sciences and the field of mental health (Money and Erhard, 1982).

Money, who worked on hermaphroditism in the Department of Child Psychiatry at John Hopkins University Hospital, was struck by what he called the gender core. He found that a hermaphrodite child's sense of their own gender (feminine or masculine) corresponded to the child's parents'belief about the sex of the body they were raising. Indeed, even when, by means of treatments or simple maturation, the biological body came to correspond to the "other sex", the child's sense of self, or gender identity, did not change. In other words, parents' or guardians' beliefs in early childhood are what inform that primary identification, beliefs that may well reflect parents' imaginaries. Looking to those findings, Robert Stoller differentiated between gender identity and sexual identity at the meeting of the International Psychoanalytic Association in Stockholm in 1963. The first term is pertinent to "those persons who have a man's body but feel like a woman" (Stoller, 1964). He used the term only to refer to male bodies—a sign of the times—but it came to be used to refer to the gender identities of both male and female bodies.

A concept that originated in child psychiatry worked its way over to the field of the social sciences. It was then appropriated by academic feminism and activism. From there, it reached many colleagues in the mental-health professions (they thought it was an advent, but it was actually a setback).[13]

On an intrapsychic level, the acquisition of gender identity begins in the process of primary identification. That first identification is with the primary caretaker of the same sex.[14] It is complementary to the ghost of "one's own sex" regarding the caretaker "of the sex one does not belong to". That identification with some aspects of the primary caregivers is at play in the construction of the ego, which from the start is gendered. In other words, "gender is one of the attributes constituent of the ego from its very origin" (Dio Bleichmar, 1996).

A child arrives at the gender ideal taken as a model not through the channel of sexuality, then, but through the channel of narcissism. It is not until later, with the resolution of the Oedipal complex, that the child acquires a sexual characteristic through a secondary identification, namely, identification with the caregiver as a sexed being. It is at that moment that the child's predominant desiring modality and choice of erotic object is determined. Neither of those later determinations is tied to a child's gender identity, which is formed earlier.

Hence, gender identity is constituted intersubjectively during early experiences of care through conscious or unconscious identification with the femininity/masculinity of those who care for the child, experiences of the child-subject's body and psyche. But, since this process is interactive (Benjamin, 1995), children identify with and take on the traits and aspects of the primary caregivers that, for some reason, interest them or capture their attention. Those are the traits or aspects drawn on to constitute the ego ideal.

That means that all primary caregivers propose identification with gender contents that, consciously or unconsciously, they project. That does not vary with trans or cis children. At the same time, however, the child engages in an active process of appropriation. Gender identity is an outgrowth of that back-and-forth between subjects (child and caregiver).

Getting back to the question of the "innate", can something that dates back to the very early constitution of the psyche also come from outside the subject? Of course, it can. Once again, we are talking here about gender identity, not sexed position.

The problem resides, in my view, in that when that something that comes from outside the subject is not as we had hoped, it would be there is a tendency to blame the desire of the parents—usually the mother—for having generated "that queer thing". If "that queer thing" comes from outside the "queer subject", someone must be blamed for it.

Let us return to the earlier argument that the right to identity is a minor issue because identity itself operates in the realm of the imaginary. That opinion is, as asserted above, generally held by a cis person, that is, one who in our socio-historical context enjoys a hegemonic position of dominance over trans people. For one who inhabits an identity that conforms, the demand of those who do not might seem illusory or based on the assessment of a self not aware of its own tendencies.

That stance depoliticises and dehistoricises the demands of transpeople by reducing them to a structural misunderstanding. The experience of gender identity and the right to legal protection of it are things of different orders, each with its own set of implications.

In any case, sexuality, always and for all of us, comes before us as a misunderstanding: words can never capture it. But its implications vary depending on the position of a subject in a social hierarchy and the social legitimacy their gender identity and sexual practice enjoy.

The debate around the problem of equity versus equality is extremely interesting, but it is formulated as a negation: the idea that equity is only available to those who are equal is tautological (Mannoni, 1985).

No less significant, those of us who practise psychoanalysis from a gender perspective have learnt from our patients that identity is by no means set or immutable. Helpful to understanding how we have reached that conclusion are theorists like Paul B. Preciado and Raewyn (Robert W.) Connell's accounts of their own transformations. Both have gone from a cis to a trans identity, and poignantly reflected on their own processes and those of others.

Thanks to their work and the work of others, we now understand that no identity is immutable. That by no means contradicts the right to social legitimacy and legal protection.

That said, the formations that arise in childhood have significant weight since childhood is the stage that witnesses the subject's constitution. But a more open conceptualisation of the psyche recognises something that clinical observation evidences: transitions can take place at any point over the course of a life. That bespeaks fluidity rather than denies the validity of earlier transitions. Any and all identities are authentic for as long as they are authentic, regardless of later mutations.

We must not lose sight of the unconscious dimension of sexuation or of the fact that sexuality comes from the Other, from tradition. There is, crucially, always an excess, a real that persists. But at stake here is not resolving the enigma that sexuality poses for any and all subjects or an attempt to rein in pleasure so that it stops rattling and unsettling the body. That is by no means what psychoanalysis from a gender perspective sets out to do. What it does intend, rather, is for the word, for something in it, to be able to quell or alleviate the extra malaise resulting from the unjust and inequitable social configurations specific to a determined socio-historical context. The basic structure that ties pleasure to becoming a subject formulates another set of debates. Those debates understand that the agitation and enigma part and parcel of sexuality cannot be resolved by identity politics or legal rights. But that understanding by no means mitigates the importance of rights to identity and everything they provide to subjects in terms of dignity and relief from excess suffering.

Butler (2004) lucidly discusses the tension between struggles for rights, on the one hand, and strategies to continue to be a desiring subject, with all the misunderstanding, enigma, and agitation that that implies, on the other. They offer the example of their support for marriage equality and their personal decision not to get married, in the time they write that piece of work, because of the impact stable and monogamous relationships have on sexual desire. Butler speaks of the importance of the right to get married in order to have the right to decide whether to get married or not. Decission made on the basis of the desire and not on the lack of the right to decide. Not to get married because you particulary considere that the love bonds have no name for you. It is by no means the same not to join an institution to which you have access as not to have access to it.

Along similar lines, Argentina's Gender Identity Law solves some problems of identity legitimacy, but not all. Lohana Berkins (2013) echoed

Butler's logic when she said that she supports the law for strategic reasons, but criticises the fact that it allows for only two identities, one male and one female.[15] Though it, of course, represents an achievement, the law does not reflect the experience of the entire trans population, much of which needs a third position or, rather, a multiplicity of nuanced positions with their attendant social, educational, and healthcare needs (Radi, 2019).

No less important is the meaning of experience, the concept of the open psyche, and being with others. When Butler (1990) argues that gender is an incessant and performed activity beyond the will of the one who performs it, he underscores the fact that one's gender is not produced alone, but always with and for the other or others. The fact that one believes one's own gender as true does not mean that one belongs to that gender; the terms that shape that gender lie outside any one of us. We are constituted by a social world that none of us has chosen (Butler, 2005).

By the same token, we may say that a lot of water has gone under the bridge since John Money described gender identity as the result of a series of intersubjective relationships between parents and close relatives and the human offspring, a back-and-forth that yields the intimate sense harboured in the psyche of being a boy or of being a girl. Money viewed that identity and its constitution as tied to the interrelationship of the child and their parents and siblings. He used that framework to explain how someone with ambiguous secondary sexual traits acquired a gender identity in accordance with how that identity had been signified by the adults closest to the child.

Today, we face a series of new challenges:

- To develop tools to support children who from a very young age are named by others in a way that differs from how they perceive themselves
- To listen respectfully when a parent states that they do not believe they wanted a daughter instead of a son or viceversa
- To respect and believe how parents present themselves, without losing sight of the fact that for all parents (regardless of whether their children are cis or trans), and indeed for all speaking subjects, the identification process is conflictive and largely unconscious
- To heed the active work of the child, who is neither a blank slate nor a passive receptor. At play in the identification process is pre-object incorporation; the process is active on the part of the child, who is not indifferent to its various aspects, but engages some rather than others
- To valorise the parents' or guardians' conscious proposals in the identification process and understand that at play in the child's operation of incorporation is not a rote copy but a translation. Between the parents' or guardians' primary identification proposal and the constitution of the subject lies a series of instances of transformation or metabolisation. In other words, there is creation and neogenesis since there is

no one-to-one reproduction of terms in the constitution of the subject
(Bleichmar, 1999)

There is a degree of truth in the assertion that it is impossible to legislate that
which erupts and persists regardless of any law. And here I look again to the
paradox Butler formulates regarding same-sex marriage, but now in relation
to eroticism versus "sexual rights" (Klein, 2000): there is no public office
where you can go to demand a right to have sex; you have to come up with
other strategies.

The name on a government-issued document cannot do away with the
malaise of a transchild, let alone guarantee them that pleasure cease to unsettle
their body over the course of their life. Gabriela Mansilla says so in no uncertain terms when she speaks of the legal right to gender identity as important
"for now". She knows that as adolescence sets in, as the penis remains, new
issues and problems will arise.[16]

Hence, though it is important to protect children from taking on the
responsibility of becoming the "heroes of a movement", they do need a social
and therapeutic response that does more than tell them to wait and see what
happens when they reach adolescence or adulthood. What is needed for each
situation must be discerned and devised. After all, these children have not
chosen to be "heroes (or victims) of a therapeutic device" either.

Major lessons learnt in clinical practice with trans children over the years
include:

- The need for interdisciplinary teams that often include school counsellors,
  administrators, and teachers; people who work at sports centres; and pae-
  diatricians, to support the families of trans children[17]
- Recognition that no matter how fervently they support their trans child,
  parents experience grief and mourning over the "loss" of a boy or girl that
  is no more
- At puberty, many girls temporarily adapt a trans male identity as a reaction to the onset of menstruation in a psychic defence mechanism against
  changes in their bodies[18]

Some Closing Reflections

Many in the mental-health field wonder whether trans people necessarily fall
into the category of psychosis as a function of "non-conformity". Here it is
important to distinguish between transidentities in children that might be considered neurotic, on the one hand, and those that might be considered psychopathological or restorative and they are in the field of psychosis according to
Meltzer's concept of mimesis as a mechanism, on the other (Blestcher, 2017).

While these conceptions help us to rescue trans people from the wholesale diagnosis of psychosis, that does not mean that there are no trans children who suffer from psychosis. And, further, that does not mean that a psychotic trans child is not really trans; in other words, it does not mean that their trans-ness is inextricably tied to their psychosis.

All of this leads to the conclusion that the vast array of transidentities and practices must be integrated into the greater human diversity.

Notes

1 Law 26743 was passed on May 9, 2012, and signed into law on May 23 of that same year.
2 In July 2010, Marriage Law 26618 was modified to enable people of the same sex to enter into a legally recognised union.
3 Law 26657.
4 The term "closet" refers to the foreclosure of public expression of people with dissident sexualities or identities for reasons of social discrimination or even the threat of violence. Coming out is when a person decides to make their diverse identity or erotic choice known in public.
5 See Mansilla (2013), Paván (2016), and Aramburu and Paván (2014). See Mansilla (2013), Paván (2016), and Aramburu and Paván (2014). Lulú is a trans girl who from a young age demanded the right to change the gender on her government-issued ID. She was able to do so in 2013, when she was just six years old. Because of chronic respiratory problems, Lulú often had to go to public hospitals for emergency treatment, where being called by the male name on her ID would send her into fits of rage and angst. In her daughter's name, Lulú's mother filed a request to change Lulú's ID, and Lulú became the first trans girl in Argentina to change her identity. This text forms part of the great debate that Lulú's case unleashed in the local psychoanalytic community.
6 See *Historias Debidas* on Canal Encuentro: https://youtu.be/eYSQGokciZ8.
7 Her father gave her an ultimatum: either you become a "real man" or you get out of here. She left.
8 That brutality is tied to the narcissistic rage that some parents experience when confronted with the image of themselves that arises in a child's transition, a transition that shatters an idealised image of the family. Transgenderism is often read as an effect of parental failure.
9 It is important to differentiate between the malaise produced by the functioning of the subject's psyche apparatus, on the one hand, and the malaise caused by a discriminatory social fabric, on the other (Meler, 2013).
10 More specifically, some versions of psychoanalysis consider universal and ahistorical one of many possible symbolic models, thus erasing any trace of context. It cannot, thus, be pegged to the patriarchal and heteronormative order that grants fathers and only fathers the symbolic function of humanising children. According to that model, heterosexuality and a gender identity that corresponds to biological sex traits are, to the exclusion of all else, "normal and desirable".
11 I would like to point out an operation whereby the symbolic order in general is mistaken for a specific symbolic order (many are possible).
12 Like Gabriela Mansilla regarding her child Lulú. See Yo nena, yo princesa (Mansilla, 2013) and the audiovisual piece with the same name (Aramburu and Paván, 2014).

13 It is interesting to reflect on this genealogy from the perspective of reception studies (García et al., 2014), which shows how some "misunderstandings" are tied to how certain concepts arrive to a given field or are appropriated by that field rather than with the concepts themselves.

14 Generally speaking, we would add today, and very likely under the heteronormative model of childrearing by a couple on the basis of the man's predominance over the woman. The coming years will show how these processes ensue in diverse contexts of childrearing.

15 Starting in 2021, though, Argentines can choose a non-binary identity on their government-issued documents.

16 She could maintain her feminine identity or become trans, or any number of other things, as Lohana Berkins recounts regarding herself. Berkins perceived herself as female as a child, but when adolescence set in and found out about trans identity, she realised that that was right for her and her way of relating to a sex organ that she was not interested in changing.

17 As pointed out by Uruguayan analyst Mauricio Clavero Lerena (2021) in the doctoral dissertation on the psychoanalysis of trans children.

18 This is only a clinical observation and should not be interpreted as if the transitions were a symptom to be resolved and not a truth of the subject to be accompanied. It shows in any case the diversity of situations of transitions in real life and their challenges for clinical devices.

References

Aramburu, M. y Paván, V. (2014) *Yo nena, yo princesa. Experiencia trans de una niña de 5 años*, disponible en: https://youtu.be/VG9V3Sba3CU

Barzani C.A. (comp.)., Leite J., Marzano M., Meler I., Osborne, R. (2015) *Actualidad de erotismo y pornografía*, Editorial Topía

Benjamin, J. (1995) *Like Subjects, Love Objects: Essays on Recognition and Sexual Difference*, Yale University Press

Berkins, L. (2013). Los existenciarios trans, en Fernandez, A.M. y Siqueira Perez, W. (comps.) *La diferencia desquiciada. Generos y diversidades sexuales,* Editorial Biblos

Bleichmar, S. (1999) *Clínica psicoanalítica y neogénesis*, Editorial Amorrortu

Blestcher, F. (2017) Infancias trans y destinos de la diferencia sexual: nuevos existenciarios, renovadas teorías, en Meler, Irene (comp.), *Psicoanálisis y género. Escritos sobre el amor, el trabajo, la sexualidad y la violencia*, Editorial Paidós

Butler, J. (1990) *Gender Trouble, Feminisim and the Subversion of Identity*, Routledge

Butler, J. (2004) *Undoing Gender*, Routledge

Butler, J. (2005) *Giving an Account of Oneself,* Fordham University Press

Castoriadis, C. (1975) *L'Institution imaginaire de la sociét.* Seuil

Clavero Lerena, M. (2021) Infancias Trans. Interpelaciones en la figura del psicoanalista. *Equinoccio, 1*(1), pp 79–100, https://doi.org/10.53693/ERPPA/1.1.6

Dio Bleichmar, E. (1996) Feminidad/masculinidad. Resistencias en el psicoanálisis al concepto de género, en Burin, Mabel y Dio Bleichmar, Emilce (comp.), *Género, psicoanálisis, subjetividad*, Editorial Paidós

Fernández, A.M. y Tajer, D. (2006) Los abortos y sus significaciones imaginarias: dispositivos políticos sobre los cuerpos de las mujeres, en Checa, S. (comp.), *Entre el derecho y la necesidad: realidades y coyunturas del aborto*, Editorial Paidós

Garcia, L., Macchioli, F., Talak, A.M., (2014) *Psicologia, niño y familia en Argentina 1900 1970. Perspectivas historias y cruces disciplinares,* Editorial Biblio
Klein, L. (2000) Del erotismo sagrado a la sexualidad científica, en Meler, I. y Tajer, D. (comps.), *Psicoanálisis y género. Debates en el Foro,* Lugar Editorial
Mannoni, O. (1985) *Clefs pour l'imaginaire ou l'Autre Scène,* Seuil
Mansilla, G. (2013) *Yo nena, yo princesa. Luana la niña que eligió su propio nombre,* UNGS
Meler, I. (2013) *Recomenzar: amor y poder después del divorcio,* Paidós
Money, J. y Erhard, A. (1982) *Desarrollo de la sexualidad humana (diferenciación y dimorfismo de la identidad de género),* Morata
Paván, V. (comp.) (2016) *Niñez trans. Experiencia de reconocimiento y derecho a la identidad,* UNGS
Radi, B. (2019) Injusticia reproductiva: entre el derecho a la identidad de género y los derechos sexuales y reproductivos, en Fundación Soberanía Sanitaria (comp.), *Salud Feminista. Soberanía de los cuerpos, poder y organización,* Editorial Tinta Limón
Sedgwick Kosofky, E. (1990) *Epistemology of the Closet,* University of California Press
Stoller, R. (1964) A Contribution to the Study of Gender Identity, *International Journal of Psychoanalysis,* N° 45 (2–3) 220–226.
Tajer, D., Reid, G., Gaba, M., Cuadra, M.E., Lo Russo, A., Salvo, I. y Solís, M. (2015) Equidad de género en la atención de la salud en la infancia, *Revista Psicoperspectivas. Individuo y Sociedad,* N° 1, Vol. 14, Santiago de Chile
Tajer, D. (2019) Prólogo, en Reid, G. (comp.), *Maternidades en tiempos de des(e)obediencias. Versiones de una clínica contemporánea,* Editorial Noveduc

Chapter 5

What Does a Man Want?

Towards the Clinical Treatment of Men from a Gender Perspective

The question "What does a man want?" is a mirrored paraphrasing of the question asked by men and repeated thousands of times during psychoanalytic training: "What do women want?" As a woman psychoanalyst, this reformulation of the question would be, I think, a much-needed step forward insofar as it interrogates the desire of the gender other than my own. But the question about male desire is not possible—for men and women alike, the enigma of female desire is still seen as a universal problem.

And that is still the case for a number of reasons.

As we have seen, socio-historical and political questions—specifically the unequal distribution of power between genders—play a fundamental role in the organisation of the psyche from a very young age. The patriarchal symbolic order that is invested with universality in relation to early-childhood relationships and childrearing has been central to the very constitution of the inner workings of our psyche on the basis of the "father solution",[1] which is in fact part of a historical construct.

The assumption that both men and women ask themselves about feminine desire, then, supports the idea that the "other gender" is always the feminine gender. It is part and parcel of the phallogocentric worldview described by Jacques Derrida in reference to the privileged status of the masculine in the construction of meaning. According to that model, there is only one symbolic order, and in it the masculine holds a monopoly on meaning, and that monopoly, in turn, is internalised in the early processes by which the psyche is formed. The problem is when that model is not seen as historical, that is, based on reigning regimes of power distribution between genders crucially operative in childrearing.

With that epistemic caveat, the question that titles this chapter serves as the springboard to address what I, as a woman analyst working from a gender perspective, see and hear in contemporary clinical practice with adult men. What I am asserting is that men *have* a gender and that my perspective, in dialogue with psychoanalysis, can make a contribution to work with male patients as they navigate the troubles they face in these times.

DOI: 10.4324/9781003411253-5

The "language bath" and ties to primordial others at play in early-childhood processes of singularisation experienced by contemporary adult men under patriarchy understood as a historical and social construct have conveyed the notion that, as men, these patients form part of a group with more social, sexual, and economic prerogatives than women, even women in the same social sector. And that, among other things, leads to specific styles of libidinal circulation and narcissism.

One mark of males' process of subjectivation as privileged subjects is a limited ability to consider some others,[2] as peers. For traditional masculine subjects, women are not considered as peers and, for that reason, men do not take the same ethical precautions in their relationships with them as they do in their relationships with other men, that is, those men they can, potentially, consider peers. That said, the list of those not worthy of human status, of the same rights that men enjoy, is long (people in other social sectors, of other races, of other sexual identities, and of other bodily abilities, to name a few). Men are less capable of empathising and of identifying with the suffering of the other if that other falls into any of those categories. Where many analysts see the psychological issues they are facing as intrapsychic in nature (questions of empathy, consideration, etc.), we as post patriarchal analysts can invite them to begin to articulate the political and the psychic in order to read information differently and to identify what types of subjects they are constituted and in what context.

Furthermore, these privileged male subjects have had to deal with "anthropological transformations" (Ayouch, 2015) that have occurred over the course of their lifetimes. The power relations between genders and how they are experienced on a daily level have shifted, creating greater freedom and pleasure but also new forms of suffering in the case of both men and women.

A whole set of trials and hardships around "masculinities" is faced by men who went through the process of subjectivation in a context of male domination (Bourdieu, 1998). They were promised a future where their monopoly on the symbolic function would be unimpeded, but they have found that promise at least partly unkept.

Turning now to clinical practice, in my office I hear the expression of *men* in the plural, rather than of a supposed universal man in the singular, and it is the plural desires of those men whom I have treated that I feel comfortable addressing.

And the first thing that comes up when that question of masculine desire resonates in my mind is the line from the tango titled *Uno* [One]: *One, full of hope, gropes for the path that his dreams promised to his longings.*

And "One" did appear—a patient who did not use the word "I" but "one". *One searches…* And the word "one", in his discourse, meant a man: "We men are like that", he would say, and that was why he was like that. In listening to him, I remembered that in masculine subjectivation under patriarchy, men often confuse personal identity with the collective identity of the male gender

(Inda, 1996)—that because the sense of belonging to that collective identity, like the identity of any hegemonic and privileged group, is conveyed starting in the cradle and relentlessly thereafter. At stake in my clinical work with One, then, was singularisation to clarify the (con)fusion of the ego, to move from the impersonal and belonging to the gender collective to subjective account-ability for his own stances as both a privileged and a suffering subject. The patient had trouble, then, going from the stance that "that's just how we men are" to asserting that that's just how *I* am. Even within that One, there was not a singular man but many men. Like so many, this future ex-husband and potentially "ex-man" (Estacikchic and Rodriguez, 1995) came to analysis pursuant to couples therapy—a common ploy to get a man who generates suf-fering in "her" but does not register his own role in that suffering to become aware of that state of affairs and be accountable for it. One thing that we psychoanalysts know is that most people who seek help are women. The men who come in are, for the most part, themselves psychologists or psychology students, sensitive men, or men who are "sent to the analyst's couch", whether by their loved ones or, in some cases of violence, by the courts.

Returning to the initial question of what a man wants, many of the men I hear in my practice say they want to do whatever it is they fancy, but at no cost. And sometimes they seek treatment because others cannot stand them, or what it is they want to do, anymore. It is common for men who seek analy-sis to say, "I am here because they can't put up with me anymore", or "I am here because they (wife, partner, children) say I cause them pain". Indeed, as mentioned above, a common strategy to get a man to start analysis is couples therapy.

One started that way. And after his partner left the couples therapy, he asked me to see him individually. In the framework of his marriage, he was turning into an "ex-man".[3] By the time he had finished his analysis, he was in another relationship. More important than those life events, though, was that once his treatment had terminated, he was using the word "I". "I am, I want, and I experience".

Many of the men I treat have trouble relating to women as subjects, that is, as "equal subjects who are also objects of love" (Benjamin, 1995), as "politi-cal peers in love" (Fernández, 1993), and as individuals with the same rights as they themselves enjoy. It is as if the only solution possible to the dilemma or tension between eroticism and tenderness were to get separated erotic life from tenderness, what Freud used to call "the degradation of the erotic life".

In his contributions to the psychology of love, Freud showed us the tension between the drives at play in the relationship to the mother, on the one hand, and to the prostitute, on the other a now dated formulation of the ongoing tension between eroticism and tenderness faced by hegemonic men in modernity. Insofar as historical, that formulation is just one of many possible modalities. Indeed, with the contemporary liberation of women's sexual practices, many women now face a similar dilemma. How can I desire a companion who is tender? How can I love my erotic object? Those dilemmas were unthinkable for women in earlier historical periods when social prohibition or what we might call the gender corset reined in these facets of female sexualities.

Men whose subjectivity corresponds to the transitional or innovative models described previously have, despite patriarchy, made some progress towards considering the love objects an equal subject. I would like to discuss how to make further progress along those lines using the clinical devices available at present, specifically the work on the psyche that, with the support of the analytic device, enables the passage from a notion of the other as the abject[4] to be expulsed and dominated to the other as enigma constituent of the self, a view conducive to solidarity. At stake is understanding that we all lead precarious lives and need one another, and we need to learn to be with others as peers, in this case with others of the other gender. For hegemonic masculinity, the abject is the feminine, the gay, the elderly, or the child. It is "that thing" that, like excrement, I must rid myself of because it connects me with my own finitude. And that is another facet of what is today called deconstructing oneself.

In the case of these men, what they seem to fear about femininity is the other who is different but similar insofar as human. In other words, they have trouble recognising women as peers, as subjects deserving of ethical consideration (Bleichmar, 2011). When they are not considered peers but subalterns, a fear of retaliation flares up, fear of revenge on the part of those exploited to breaking point because—after all—they are there to serve. Some men are harsh with women but loyal friends to other men, fellow members of the gentlemen's club that is, in their view, life itself. These are some of the exquisite paradoxes at play in the relationships between genders under contemporary (hetero)sexual patriarchy.

Other questions to explore are how the malaises endured by men today are expressed and how psychoanalysis should intervene on those malaises. And it is here that the temptation to gear treatment towards a conservative restoration of male gender privileges in order to soo the a nervous episode because "men are an endangered species" must be resisted.

Discourses that propose the bolstering of masculine power as the solution to the challenges faced by men today are problematic to say the least (Tort, 2015). As pointed out before, the premise that the end of patriarchy is the end of the world and of humanisation rests on a collective and self-centred fear: the threat of a world without us at its core. What is actually underway is nothing more and nothing less than a democratisation and redistribution of the symbolic function. The same logic informs frightened discourses— discourses also designed to frighten—that tie high rates of juvenile delinquency not to unequitable societies and youth unemployment but to the absence of the father figure. Those discourses hold that the institutionalisation of youth is a means for at-risk young people to incorporate "the symbolic order". The fact of the matter is that the version of the father figure found at many of those institutions is more like the leader of a "primitive mob"[5] than a subject who has incorporated the symbolic order and is, hence, capable of contributing to the formation of a psyche that can build social ties. I am not going to dwell here on what youths end up "incorporating" at those institutional spaces. News stories about cases of sexual and institutional abuse at them, even at the hands of the police,[6] speak for themselves.

Getting back to men in analysis, men who, generally speaking, do not represent the "hard core" of patriarchy (Connel, 1997)—after all, seeking treatment implies at least some degree of questioning of the self—I turn to the case of "Two". Two says that he needs to return to "a warm home" in the evening and gets angry with his partner when she fails to provide it. She explains that as a girl she never had "a warm home waiting for her". He did, but someone else was feeding that hearth—namely, his mother. And that was how he learnt that a warm home is lovely, but keeping it warm is "women's work". He expected his partner to do something she did not know how to do. And as a result, they were both freezing to death.

As a psychoanalyst with a gender perspective, my intervention was geared to helping him take on the task of making his home a warm place for him, his partner, and—later—their children through the reservoir of identification with that mother who was so skilled at taking care of him. He would complain, "I support us. With the money I bring home, she should be able to make sure our lives go smoothly, with food on the table, clothes ironed, and so on…".

With that Two, dissatisfied, started treatment; the couple still did not have any children. He would respond to her impossibilities, the result of losing her parents at a young age, with symbolic violence that even verged on physical violence at times. Thanks to psychoanalysis, he no longer responds violently. After a great deal of work, Two—now the father of two small children—has been able to accept that she is not "the woman of his dreams" but a real woman with whom he can live. It has not been easy, but to a large extent he has assumed that someone (in this case, he) has to step up, gender roles be damned. After all, he is the only one of the two capable of performing those tasks because he had a caring mother with whom to identify. In short, he is the one who knows how to do these things. He was overwhelmed by angst before the sense of emasculation he experienced when he began to identify with his mother, but he was able to work through those feelings. Indeed, today he takes pride and comfort in bearing the traits of his esteemed mother. He recently told me that he considers himself a recovered "male chauvinist". I cherish his statement that "the kid I was when I was eighteen would bully the man I am today".

When "Three" came to my office, he had suddenly come up against the costs of "doing what he wanted". He sought treatment when, at the same time, both his wife and his lover had become pregnant. His brave lover, a colleague, recommended an analyst with a gender perspective because she trusted that such an analyst would be able to position all of them as subjects. She also trusted in the decision he would make pursuant to that repositioning.

In his analysis, Three realised that the fundamental decision he had to make was whom to choose as his life partner and what position he would take before the two children on the way. He decided to stay with his wife and act as a parent of the child conceived in that relationship. After that choice was made, his lover decided to end the relationship except in the strictly professional sphere (they worked at the same establishment) and have an abortion without including him in the process. When Three decided to terminate analysis, he had taken responsibility for his decisions—the angst they brought him had been alleviated. He was able to connect the situation he found himself in with his father, who had had parallel partners as his mother and he himself, as the son of that union, suffered in silence.

"Four", a university student in Buenos Aires from an affluent family from a conservative Argentine province, was deeply stricken and afraid because an ex-girlfriend, who was from his home province, had shamed him on the social networks for having treated her badly. He admitted that she was right—he had not, in fact, treated her well. But he said he had since changed. Living in Buenos Aires, which is a different milieu, and having feminist friends had enabled him to "deconstruct" his hegemonic masculinity. He was ashamed and afraid of not being able to restore his image in his home province, where he wanted to spend the holidays. Furthermore, he wanted to be a musician and thought that having been shamed would interfere with his career. He pointed to a number of cases of male singers who had been condemned for sexist behaviour. We talked about the possibility that he wrote to his ex-girlfriend to apologise for how he had behaved towards her, explaining that only recently, after having discovered new forms of gender relations, had he realised how badly he had treated her. He asked himself what he would do if she did not answer him and was able to understand that insisting would be a form of harassment. In developing that response to the situation, he spoke of his father's sexism; it was from him he had learnt how to be little and degrade women, but that is not how he wants to act going forward.

When "Five" came in for treatment, he was a gay man who for over 15 years had been unable to establish loving sexual relationships with men he found attractive—his despair over that situation was the reason he sought treatment. He also had trouble keeping a job even though he was a highly qualified language teacher; he would get embroiled in workplace disputes. His parents had been separated for many years, and he was very close to his mother, a woman with a strong character. His relationship with his father, who was very generous with Five, was distant. Indeed, both he and his mother disdained him. We worked on those relationships, helping him separate from his mother and explore if he might find something of value in that father. In general, Five—like his mother—was scornful of men and masculinity. Over the course of analysis, Five started frequenting gay clubs and porn movie houses. He discovered at the clubs that he enjoyed doing himself up as a woman. From that position, he was able to be with men whom he found attractive.

He started to wax his body hair. Although the process was painful, he was finally pleased with his own image. He was much more comfortable with himself now than when he had started treatment, but he picked up on the fact that I as an analyst was not prepared at that time to help him through the transition.[7] He thanked me for everything and told me he would look for another analyst more experienced in what he was going through. It was not until much later that I was able to understand what he had wanted to convey to me. I also learnt that he is now a trans woman. I did not, at that time, have the theory required to accompany him. While it is true that he had scorn for masculinity, and that was something we worked on, that work was not what he needed to be able to pursue his vital desire and identity. The analyst that I am today, unlike the one I was 15 years ago when I was working with Five, knows that scorn for masculinity and the desire to cross dress or even transition can coexist without a necessary line of causality.

What does a man want? Should we keep asking the poets? Or are we contemporary psychoanalysts up to the challenges that our socio-historical juncture puts before us regarding new modes of pleasure and suffering among men?

Notes

1 This is a concept theorised by French psychoanalyst Michel Tort in his book Fin du dogme paternel (2005). It addresses how, at a historical moment that has witnessed the decline in the power of men, psychoanalysis has restored that power by formulating that, thanks to its intrapsychic weight, the paternal figure is the only one with the resources to resolve the Oedipal complex. In sum, that recent psychoanalytic thinking sees the role that men have played because of the historical power granted to them by patriarchy as a psychic invariable..

2 Been seen as subaltern people related to gender, race, sexual option, and social class.

3 I mean as an ex-man the fact that his wife didn't see him as a partner just a "husband".

4 In Gender Trouble..., Butler (1990) looks to Julia Kristeva's notion of the abject as a paradigm to grapple with gender. In Powers of Horror: An Essay on Abjection, Kristeva (1982) uses the word "abject" to name bodily excesses, that which is expelled and discarded (feces, urine, vomit, tears, and saliva). The abject body is the one we do not want to see in ourselves: our excrement and excesses and, in the end, our corpse—our abject body is our disease and our death. A society's abject bodies are the ones it excretes the way our bodies excrete their excesses or that which causes us to decay until we finally die. Butler brings the concept of the abject to bear on the vulnerability of transexual, transvestite, transgender, and intersex persons vis-à-vis gender norms, as well as of disabled persons vis-à-vis other norms. Butler argues that the explanation for the hate and violence in response to differences in identity, sexuality, and functionality is that those differences remind us that our bodies will age and we will die; that is, the deficient body reminds us of the repugnant finitude of our own abjection and of our own death (Porchat, 2015).

5 Freud uses this concept in Group Psychology and the Analysis of the Ego to describe the myth of the totemic, authoritarian, and arbitrary father not inscribed in the symbolic order. In that myth, the father, who is positioned as the law onto himself, is murdered by his sons as a way to democratise relationships between men.

6 I personally know two people, each with an adolescent male from marginalised social classes in their family who, once in such institutions, were not brought into the symbolic order but rather recruited by the guards at those institutions to commit crimes for them. In both cases, the young men died early and unexplained deaths.

7 A reflection I came upon recently in a text by Paul B. Preciado (2022) caused me to re-examine the countertransference I had experienced with that patient. Preciado states his impression that "the bodily, erotic, and sexual experience of the trans-gender person generates an irrepressible anguish in the analyst … who is not up to the challenge of looking at a body beyond their own cis and heterosexual experience, beyond their own conventions of gender and sex" (p.89). Personally, I believe that my own feminist questioning of the aesthetic models of traditional femininity did me and my patient a disservice regarding his—that was the pronoun the patient at the time—decision to go through the painful process of waxing all his body hair. His assumption of traditional feminine models of beauty was beyond the limit at that time for what I could accompany and listen to. Experiences in subsequent years have allowed me to change that. I understand Preciado's observation as an invitation for analysts to re-examine our countertransference vis-à-vis everyone who comes in for treatment, and I, in turn, invite us not to understand that which we hear according to the parameters of convention or supposition. After all, we cannot assume that whiteness, cis-ness, or heterosexuality is inhabited the same way by everyone—and that holds true for analysts as well, though as analysts we must re-examine the marks of hegemony and supremacy that those categories bear. Similarly, transness, homosexuality, and brownness are inhabited in countless ways, if always in a framework of inequality.

References

Ayouch, T. (2015) *Géneros, Cuerpos y Placeres. Perversiones psicoanáliticas con Michel Foucault,* Editorial Letra viva

Benjamin, J. (1995) *Like Subjects, Love Objects: Essays on Recognition and Sexual Difference,* Yale University Press

Bleichmar, S. (2011) *La construcción del sujeto ético,* Editorial Paidós

Bourdieu, P. (1998) *La Domination masculine,* Seuil

Butler, J. (1990) *Gender Trouble, Feminisim and the Subversion of Identity,* Routledge

Connel, R.W. (1997) La organización Social de la Masculinidad, en Valdés, Teresa y Olavarría, José (eds.), *Masculinidad/es. Poder y Crisis,* Ediciones de las Mujeres

Estacikchic, R. y Rodriguez, S., (1995) *Pollerudos. Destinos de la sexualidad masculina,* Ediciones Odisea

Fernández, A.M. (1993) *La Mujer de la ilusión. Pactos y contratos entre hombres y mujeres,* Editorial Paidós

Inda, N. (1996) Género Masculino, Número Singular, en Burín, Mabel y Dio Bleichmar, Emilce (comps.), *Género, Psicoanálisis y Subjetividad.* Editorial Paidós

Kristeva, J. (1982) *Powers of horror: an essay on abjection,* Columbia UP

Preciado, P.B. (2022) *Yo soy el monstruo que os habla. Informe para una academia de psicoanalistas,* Anagrama

Porchat, P. (2015) Um corpo para Judith Butler, *Revista Periódicus, 1* (3), pp. 37–51, https://doi.org/10.9771/peri.v1i3.14254

Tort, M. (2005) *Fin du dogme paternel,* Flammarion, Aubier

Tort, M. (2015) *Las subjetividades patriarcales. Un psicoanálisis incierto en las transformaciones históricas,* Editorial Topia

Chapter 6

Amphibians

Sexuality and Love in Contemporary Women and Their Clinical Challenges

This chapter discusses situations that contemporary women bring to psychoanalytic practice, situations that evidence the new challenges and conflicts both feminism and persistent patriarchy pose for experiences of love and desire. It also presents some possible clinical interventions offered by psychoanalysis from a gender perspective.

First, though, we must reflect on how the current configuration of love and sex has affected clinical work with women, regarding specifically two major historical novelties: women as subjects with rights and desires, and a psychoanalysis from a gender perspective capable of listening to them.

At stake in clinical work with contemporary women are new freedoms, but also new dilemmas or, at least, dilemmas that had been expressed in different terms as practices once unavailable to women due to internalised age-old prohibitions have emerged. Once again, I am interested in articulating socio-historical factors with intersubjective and intrapsychic factors. I will describe real subjects and how they navigate the dynamics of their own psyche and those of others, mindful of the fantasy of the other each one of us creates. Relevant to this analysis is the category of generation. I have used it in other texts (Tajer, 2020a) to indicate those who inhabit the same time period, with its specific ways of living life, regardless of divergent individual tendencies. The concept stands against any idea of universalisation; it must not be applied wholesale to singular subjectivities.

The generation of women whose cases are explored in this chapter are between the ages of 25 and 45. They are city-dwellers, and most of them have been influenced by feminism, though to varying degrees. Their employment situations and educational backgrounds vary, but they are all economically self-sufficient. The women under the age of 35 do not have children, and each of the women older than that has one child born during a relationship to a man that lasted between five and ten years.

Elsewhere (Tajer, 2020b) I pointed out that women today face a tension that was until just a few years ago the sole terrain of men, namely how **to love the one you desire and desire the one you love**. That dilemma seems to arise with greater freedom and access to rights in the spheres of love and

DOI: 10.4324/9781003411253-6

sex. Until recently, women called on men, who enjoyed greater prerogative in those spheres, to be "affectively accountable" for how that tension between love and sex and its expression affected their partners.

Now women must be affectively accountable as well as they work out the tension between tenderness, love, and attachment, on the one hand, and eroticism, on the other, and the difficulty in experiencing all of those things with one person. At first, how women deal with that tension *appears* to differ little from how men do. But that is just how it seems. In fact, even though women have gained sexual and affective freedom and rights, patriarchy—delegitimised though it may be—is alive and well; it still leaves its unequal marks on genders.

The erotic and amorous practices of the women analysands presented here differ from the heteronormative; they attempt—and sometime manage—to elude patriarchy and the mandate of monogamy, which fell solely on women under modernity. Defying patriarchy also means re-signifying the practices of motherhood and the contexts in which reproductive projects take shape.

Regarding their sexuality, these women have sex with men and women, and neither of those object choices defines their identity. Indeed, for them these practices cannot be placed in pat categories.

In listening to these women talk about their lives, I have not heard them speak of periods in the closet. They describe, rather, an array of experiences they have had since adolescence in what might be called an open or fluid sexuality. I would call them amphibian sexualities. Indeed, in this chapter I refer to these women themselves as amphibians.

These amphibians circulate at a socio-historical juncture where, as stated above, normative and hierarchical heterosexuality continues to be dominant. In their heterosexual practices with men, these women have visions and expectations linked to the asymmetrical norms at play in that kind of heterosexuality, as well as frustrations born of that same model. They grant the man they are with the power to validate their existence and confirm their worth— indeed, they expect them to do so—even though that stance runs counter to their ideals and aspirations of equality. In other words, they narcissistically expect men to validate them while also idealising those men insofar as they occupy a position they themselves aspire to reach, in a dynamic where men have a power over them that they do not hold over men. Despite sexual and amorous ideals and practises that include open relationships, polyamory, and fluidity in the choice of erotic object, these women's processes of subjectivation took place according to the paradigm of dominant heterosexuality, which they internalised at a very young age.

No life is devoid of problems or conflicts, and I will present here some of the problems and conflicts I have witnessed in clinical work with the lives of contemporary women with a specific set of characteristics. The key questions these women ask themselves at the contemporary juncture are: Who am I? Whom am I attracted to? What do I want from love and from sex?

I will present some vignettes from my clinical work with these women that exemplify the centrality of those questions.

One

One's preferred sex partners are men, and she has enjoyed intense sexual experiences with a number of them, but she cannot tolerate an affective relationship with a man because she is very sensitive to everyday sexist micro-aggressions. As a grown woman, she had her first stable relationship with a woman whom she loves and who loves and supports her but with whom she does not experience the same sexual intensity. The two women agreed to be monogamous.

One agreed to monogamy because of how much she values feeling supported and protected. But her sexual desire is not entirely satisfied by her relationship. Be that as it may, she has not decided to follow the traditional masculine model and satisfy those two needs—the need for love and the need for sex—with two different people.

Two

After a first romantic relationship with a woman, she had a relationship with a man several years older than her whom she idealised intellectually. When she first came in for treatment, she had a number of freelance jobs in her field but was just making ends meet. She decided to move out of her family home. Though he initially invited her to move in with him, Two's partner let her know in a thousand different ways that he was not really up for cohabitation. Two got the message.

After working on the issue in analysis, Two decided to move out on her own. Not long after, she found a steady job in her field that provided rich opportunities for professional growth. She was finally able to live comfortably from just one job. In different ways, her boyfriend undermined her new job because she was less available. One month after she got the job, he proposed opening up their relationship. Two months later and after a number of scenes where he snubbed Two, he decided to end the relationship because "highly" eroticised by another woman.

Two is devastated. She says she cannot imagine life without him. At the same time, the level of eroticism and intellectual esteem in her life soars without him. She has sex with women and with other men for the first time. (That former partner was the first and only man she had had sex with, which meant she gauged what she experienced sexually with men in general solely on the basis of her experience with him.) She finds the experiences with these other men very satisfying, and at the same time she pursues sex with women.

Three

Three is another amphibian in sex and love who claims no interest in living with a partner. The model she upholds is living with women friends (she idealises bonds between women). She claims that the decision to live with women friends is a choice, one option among many, not a way to get by when unpartnered.

According to Three's idealisation of "sisterhood", women are by definition mutually supportive. But the reality of cohabitation soon dispels that illusion. Rivalry, competition, class hatred, intolerance, and pre-Oedipal forms of relating soon rear their head. Those of us who work in psychoanalysis from a gender perspective know that pre-Oedipal dynamics of attachment and difficulty in differentiation are often at play in groups of women in what has been called "the identicals" (Amorós Puente, 1985; Fernández, 1993). In the model of the identicals, there is an illusion of symmetry; all of the women in the group should be equal; if anyone stands out or differs in any way, it is experienced as a threat to the tie. That phenomenon is also evident when women choose a male rather than a female delegate or representative in the groups of which they form part.

For clinical work, the fact that a bond takes that "identical" form does not indicate the need to "go toward the Oedipal resolution" conceived as a superior or more evolved stage. According to that view, a break in the mother-child dyad ushers in legality in a conception that sees attachment as evidence of lawlessness. More appropriate clinical intervention fosters singularisation by means of mutual recognition, rather than through rejection or relegation of the other in a break in the relationship (Benjamin, 1995). Along these lines, I would further argue that the figure of Narcissus is no less structural to the psyche than the figure of Oedipus (Levinton Dolman, 2000). Indeed, neither is more important than the other, and that must be kept in mind when deciding how to treat these attachments in clinical practice.

Four

Four is an amphibian who has fulfilling sexual and love relationships with men and women, though lately her preference has been for women. She is not interested in a monogamous relationship, but rather in an open or polyamorous tie. At the same time, she would like more attention from X, her primary partner. And that is not an easy request to make since X began exploring polyamory through their relationship, not before, and it has been a real awakening for her.

Four is committed to their agreement and the pleasures it affords, even though she feels jealous, excluded, and genuine interest in X's other partners as people.

She is startled by these feelings. She believes there is a model exempt from this type of conflict, a model she believes holds the key to happiness. In her psychoanalysis, we have worked on the idea that every model brings its own set of problems. Freedom resides in the ability to choose which set of problems one wants to grapple with.

Recently, she has decided **she only wants to spend energy on her own conflicts; she does not want to waste time thinking about what is going on in the mind of someone else, in this case X.** She speaks of that "very traditional feminine" role of asking oneself time and again what the other person wanted to say, of having to decode the other's desire. Her decision to turn away from all that has proven very rewarding.

Five

Five is a trans man who transitioned after having lived as a heterosexual and feminist cis woman. He says that most of his relationships are with heterosexual cis women, feminists who like men in bed but cannot tolerate their patriarchal attitudes and behaviours. That is the population with whom he finds fulfilling sexual and romantic relationships.

Six

A 40-year-old cis woman who, in the framework of a relationship where the couple does not live together, decides to have a child. Her male partner supports her, and they establish an arrangement where the three of them spend some days together and others apart.

Seven

A cis woman over the age of 30 begins psychoanalysis to decide whether to become a mother. She lives with her male partner, but they agree that the relationship is not suited to raising a family together.

Over the course of her analysis, they decide to move into separate homes but stay together. In analysis, Seven begins to invert her thinking: her primary desire is to become a mother; she will then figure out what to do with the relationship and whether to live with her partner and child. She gets pregnant and, to her surprise, the couple stays together.

Some Closing Remarks

I have been struck in my clinical practise by the number of young amphibians who are very brilliant intellectually while inhibited in the sexual field. Relevant to that is, in my view, a historical context that idealises very active and free sexuality. Indeed, that often operates more as a mandate than as an expression of a subject's desire. The contrast between the intellectual and sexual spheres is heightened by a super-ego that condemns these women's sexuality as feeble by the standards they have incorporated. The calm required for sexual exploration is done a disservice by a highly critical assessment on the part of these amphibians of their ability to meet ideals; they find themselves gauging the performance and success of sexual practises that must develop over time, over the course of an encounter or various encounters. At play in much of my clinical work with these women is helping them to tame those critical voices so that they can experience the process of getting to know themselves and their sexuality.

I appreciate that clinical interventions along these lines are possible at a historical moment critical of the idea of one "true" sexuality and affectivity that applies to everyone. There is more room for each subject to construct and experience their own sexuality, a sexuality that better reflects what each subject is and wants for themselves.

I have not observed the inhibition described above in older amphibians with more sexual experience. Perhaps that is because they came of age in more restrictive contexts that paradoxically spared them the social pressure to have a very active sex life from early on. They were able to explore at as lower pace.

Something else that has struck me about the amphibians is their relationships to their parents, some of whom are quite elderly. Because, in its early days, COVID-19 posed such a danger to the elderly, it made face-to-face encounters with older parents difficult if not impossible, thus widening the distance between generations I had detected in my clinical practise.

I have observed that younger amphibians have the sense that they enjoy greater freedom and broader rights with their peers than with their parents. Furthermore, they deem themselves entitled to those rights and freedoms but do not grant them to their parents. I had noticed this before the pandemic, though the pandemic only heightened the tendency.

These women see themselves as having a great many rights and very few responsibilities in their intergenerational bonds. They valorise relationships based on affinity and tend to dismiss solidarity with those who took care of them when they were children. Furthermore, as one of the amphibians put it,

> I am part of a generation that does not imagine itself growing old with a life partner they have been with for decades. Relationships come and go. The only thing you can count on is the family you were born into.

Striking here is the assumption that others are the source of stability; there is no notion of reciprocity, of providing stability to those others. It could even be said that they do not believe in reciprocity or that relationships based on affinity can be stable—that despite their commitment to those relationships.

This panorama suggests a very complex future scenario where neoliberal values of individualism yield a model based on affinity to the detriment of reciprocal accountability over the course of a lifetime.[1]

Also of note with this group of women is the independence of procreation and stable partnerships where the two members live together. Different affective and family configurations begin to take shape at a historical moment when being a mother has ceased to be a social mandate. The desire to be or not to be a mother is one desire amongst many rather than a synonym for feminine fulfilment. It is thus becoming possible to distinguish the desire to have a life partner from the desire to have a child; having a child is no longer envisioned as a way to keep a relationship together. Nor is it mandatory to live in the same household as the person with whom you have children, the person who is also your romantic partner.

Looking to the model of bisexual dominance among Greek male citizens, a model Foucault studied, I would say, in closing, that contemporary amphibians' **undominance bisexuality** must be understood in relation to a still operative patriarchy coupled with the decline of the modern sexual order.

Note

1 A phrase I came up with and shared on the social networks captures this tension: polyamory, or open relationships, plus patriarchy is neoliberalism in relationships. Under the guise of equality, those with greater power on the market of love and sex because "beautiful", able-bodied, or young, for instance, enjoy greater success.

References

Amorós Puente, C. (1985) *Hacia una crítica de la razón patriarcal.* Anthropos

Benjamin, J. (1995) *Like Subjects, Love Objects: Essays on Recognition and Sexual Difference*, Yale University Press

Fernández, A.M. (1993) *La mujer de la ilusión.* Paidós

Levinton Dolman, N. (2000) *El superyó femenino. La moral en las mujeres*, Biblioteca Nueva.

Tajer, D. (dir.) (2020a) *Niñez, adolescencia y género. Herramientas Interdisciplinarias para equipos de salud y educación*, Noveduc

Tajer, D. (2020b) *Psicoanálisis para todxs. Por una clínica pospatriarcal, posheteronormativa y poscolonial.* Topía Editorial

Conceptualising the Relationship between Subjectivity, Power, Psychoanalysis, and Gender[1]

This chapter discusses Silvia Bleichmar's[2] contributions to understanding the relationship between the social and the subjective on both inter- and intra-subjective level and the impact of those contributions on how psychoanalysis from a gender perspective conceives power relations. It includes as well her contributions to notions of masculinities, femininities, and sexual and identity diversities in psychoanalysis.

In Bleichmar's thinking, the relationship between politics and psychoanalysis revolves around at least four axes:

1   Subjects' relationships with power
2   Public space as the space of the polis
3   Public space as the space of the state. This perspective understands the state as a presence that regulates and redistributes social and economic inequalities
4   The possibility of change and reorganizasion within psychoanalysis in what she called "upholding paradigms by casting off ballasts" (2005)

I will explore three lines of her work to exemplify how those four axes contribute to psychoanalytic theory and practice.

On the articulation of politics, history, and the constitution of the psyche

The notions of the **production of subjectivity** and the **constitution of the psyche** (2005) are interrelated in Bleichmar's work.

At play in the **production of subjectivity** is the relationship between the representations that a given society institutes for the formation of subjects authorised to circulate within that society, on the one hand, and how each subject constitutes their singularity, on the other. Regarding that second concept, the **constitution of the psyche**, in her thinking, the determination of psyche's suffering is libidinal.

DOI: 10.4324/9781003411253-7

From Bleichmar's perspective, those two notions are integral to the constitution of the psyche's apparatus. In other words, that apparatus is not formed pursuant to the influence or impact of something external.

The socio-historical and the political are, for Bleichmar, fundamental to the psyche's organisation from the very outset. She refuses to use the word "culture" to refer to the socio-historical[3] or to envision the outside world as a mere stage on which subjectivity unfolds. The traditional assumption is that the subject's motivations mostly originate in the intra-psychic realm or, at times, in the inter-subjective realm. To conceptualise her distance from those assumptions, she introduced the notion of "desiring spiritualism".[4] That term refers to the operation of those who conceive of the constitution of the psyche as the introduction of the child into "the" symbolic order, presumed to be universal. That introduction, it is further presumed, takes place in childrearing, in the child's early relationships. That vision reproduces a family-centred perspective: the main determinant of the process of subjectivation are parental desires for the subject to come.

The notion of "desiring spiritualism" entails a harsh critique of the conceptions of pre-citizenry or para-citizenry. Those conceptions upheld by many psychoanalysts negate the tie between bodies and psyches, on the one hand, and between psyches and history and legal frameworks, on the other. That said, Bleichmar by no means believed in what she called a sociologist vision where the subject is seen as a carbon copy of the social (a vision outlined in Chapter 3). Bleichmar rejected both that sociologist fallacy and its antithesis, which might be called the subject-as-island fallacy described above.

Her work articulates a critique of universality as a given, as an unquestioned and equal starting point for all of us.[5] For Bleichmar, universality is a utopia or possible point of arrival. She ascribed to the best of the modern tradition, defending universality as equality under the law and criticising states of exception—from fascism to state terrorism and neoliberalism—that set up a double standard for subjects (I will discuss that further in relation to the problem of exclusion and the peer).

For that reason, her seminars always began with remarks on reality, on the surrounding context. Reality was not a hindrance to be quickly overcome to get to the point, but rather something to grapple with and elucidate together. The collective discussion of political events at the beginning of each class cast away the notion that psychoanalysis is a fiction to be transmitted, like a movie or play, only once the lights are out. She understood transmission in psychoanalysis as a fictional method that was, nonetheless, very close to a life science.

That was the context for her enthusiasm about the political changes that took place after 2003,[6] which she described in some detail in her book *No me hubiera gustado morir en los 90*,[7] published in 2007. She was encouraged by the new horizons in the social and subjective tissue partly sutured after the devastation of neoliberalism in the 1990s. More specifically, rights were restored, even expanded, and the economy reactivated. Perhaps more importantly, there was once again room for hope. Bleichmar believed that all of that had an impact on the psyche. Subjects could once again devise projects and feel part of a social whole—conditions fundamental to the confirmation of the value of their existence. In exclusive socioeconomic models of the types endured both in the 1990s and, fundamentally, during the dictatorship in power from 1976 to 1983, the fate of many mattered not at all.

The subject, for Bleichmar, is situated. She is a citizen who participates in the social contract. At the same time, they have an unconscious—he doesn't know everything about himself. And social inclusion is one of the conditions necessary for the psyche to unfold—a notion that feminist psychoanalysis looks to when it questions holding women subjects accountable for violence delivered upon them as second-class citizens compared to their male counterparts (see Chapter 3).

Her conception of citizenship also informed her use in clinical practice of what, in the sphere of public health, are called patient's rights—a framework almost unheard of in the practices of contemporary psychoanalysts, where their relationships with patients are virtually non-contractual. They do not see that psychoanalytic treatment entails, along with so much else, a contract; they view its terms as natural, as the rules of the game, something like a dress code. What Bleichmar pointed out is as simple as it is important: the "house rules" must always be established at the outset. It is never safe to assume that the other person knows them. Nothing should be taken for granted. For example, according to what criteria should increases in fees be calculated—a key question in a country like Argentina, which has historically experienced spells of very high inflation. What happens when a patient doesn't show up? Is a make-up session scheduled? Are fees paid during the psychoanalyst's vacation? The answer is that everything must be spelt out at the beginning, and then the rules must be respected by both parties. And that brings to the table the question of ethics underlying any contract. That question is fundamental to protecting the analysand from possible abuses at the hand of the analyst since the relationship between them is by nature asymmetrical and the vulnerability of the analysand part of parcel of the analytic device.

Her theoretical work and her clinical practice, then, evidence concern with how to understand the question of subjective accountability considering unequal vulnerabilities due to power asymmetries, whatever their origin may be. In the clinical device, the patient is the one with less power; in cross-generational relationships, it is the younger generation (something Bleichmar, as a psychoanalyst who treated children, was keenly aware of); in social relationships, it is the marginalised, women, lgttb* people, the poor, political prisoners, racialised people, and many others.

She also addressed how to begin clinical work in cases where the psyche has been traumatised in contexts of inequality.[8] First, the analyst must be available as a witness who can take in in a hospitable fashion the patient's account of the horror they experienced, knowing that they will be believed

(García Reinoso, 1998). Afterwards, and only afterwards, comes the time to undertake the process of constructing subjective accountability. Analysts, as ethical subjects, must take measures against to re-victimise the victims.

Her production also addresses how to work with subjects that *do* have power, that is, hegemonic subjects that seek treatment. Regarding that, she speaks of the "ethicalisation" of the subject in analysis. I have looked to that concept in my work from a gender perspective with hegemonic males[9] as well as my work on the health costs of hegemonic masculinity, specifically greater vulnerability to coronary disease (Tajer, 2009).

To illustrate this, I will recount an anecdote. I once sent her as a patient a fellow psychoanalyst, a man in whom I had witnessed sexist attitudes and abuse of his prerogatives as a hegemonic subject. Silvia proved very helpful. We were talking about something else one day when she changed the topic. "That guy you sent me—he's a good person. He does what he does because he can't do anything else". That did not mean she supported his actions or attitudes, but that in him she had found an ethical subject. He did not intend to do harm even when he ended up doing it. And that was a starting point, a basis from which to work towards a change in position—which is, in fact, what happened.

That was, for me, an excellent lesson on how to deal with power asymmetries, in that case between genders, and on how to work with both those who endure the suffering and those who cause it—provided, of course, those who cause it are willing to be held accountable. That twofold effort is useful to mending past harm.

Another relevant question is how to include reality, or Freud's principle of reality, in clinical intervention.

I remember one wonderful intervention that I often have occasion to use myself in my own practice. Bleichmar was treating a woman over the age of 60 who, when her mother died, referred to herself as an orphan. She intervened, saying that "after a certain age, one is no longer an orphan", differentiating between the suffering occasioned by the loss of a parent at any age and the vulnerability that young children who lose their parents face. Perceiving oneself as an orphan at an advanced age indicates an ongoing infantile attachment to parents. If not worked through, that poses the risk of ageing without having matured.

On the question of the peer and the impact of social inclusion: Bios and Zoe

Bleichmar wrote two phrases uncannily relevant to these times:

- Ingenuity is not a virtue, and political ingenuity means a lack of accountability.
- Those who hoped the thief would return their riches have conceded to turning their life into a plaything of the gods.

Those two statements can be understood in terms of the concepts of exclusion, the field of the peer, bios, and zoe—the corner stones of Bleichmar's work.

At play in her intellectual production is the idea that the peer as concept and as realm encompasses humanity as a whole. Society works better when it is characterised by social inclusion, and it is marked by pain when social exclusion reigns—regardless of who experiences it—hence the name of her book *Dolor país* [*Country Pain*].

In that book, she draws a significant distinction from what we might call a limited or low-intensity conception of the peer.

Bleichmar asks who our peers are. Who is a peer[10] to each one of us?

And she responds that there are at least two different answers to that question, each one with its own set of implications: our peers are humanity as a whole; our peers are those seen as forming part of the same social group (our neighbours, our ethnic or cultural group, fellow members of a club, fellow women, fellow men, and so forth).

On the basis of that distinction, I have been able to develop notions pertinent to the relationships between men and women under patriarchy. For men who have become subjects according to the hegemonic model, their peers are other men. Women are, for them, objects to enjoy in an ethical double standard.[11] Of course, this is not expressed explicitly by hegemonic males—they are often unaware of it. But that logic underlies their actions.

Once the field of peers has been established, whether consciously or unconsciously and regardless of whom is included or excluded, rules are established regarding what can be done to and with peers and what can be done to and with those not seen as peers.

Examples of what happens when the field of peers is limited and exclusive include Nazism, state terrorism in Argentina and elsewhere, racism and neo-liberalism. In those models, the lives of non-peers do not matter at all.

Part and parcel of an exclusive definition of the peer is a legal framework of segregation[12] (the concentration camp, the mental institution, apartheid, etc.). Segregation is necessary to delimit a portion of the territory outside the "normal" judicial order—the place to which the excluded are confined. Anyone who ends up in that territory can be subject to any class of treatment pursuant to a state of exception or differential rights (Agamben, 2003). That is what is at stake in racial laws as well as the loss (or gain, as the case may be) of broad social rights redefined as "charity" only for the "deserving poor". A similar logic informs judicial "mental competency" proceedings and guardianship of minors, women, and the elderly.

For all of these reasons, I believe the enactment in Argentina of laws sanctioning an individual's right to determine their own gender identity and to make their own mental health decisions is so important. These are tools to combat "states of exception" as well as what I might call actions of exception that violate rights and ruin lives.

And that entire legal and social framework acts on clinical practice. Silvia warned time and again that the loss of the notion of collectivity (country, humanity) means the inability to identify with the suffering of the other. Whereas some see only psychological issues and intra-psychic challenges like the inability to empathise, and others toss what is actually a complex problem affecting all realms of individual and collective life into the large sack of "postmodernism" or "the liquid"—categories that explain everything and nothing at all—she articulated the political and the psychological. The question is what subject one can be in what context—a conception that entails a critique of the "good Samarian".[13]

This framework enables us to understand how someone might want democracy for themselves yet be authoritarian with others—namely, by not recognising that that other, or those others, is a fellow subject. It enables us to understand how privileged subjectivities and subjectivities with impunity take shape in exclusive societies. These concepts form the basis from which I have created tools for my own practice in order to understand the impact of privileged subjectivity and its construction in gender relations. The framework could be adjusted to address the complexity at play in intersectionality.

Indeed, these concepts are useful, in my view, not only as tools for clinical intervention in situations of inequality, but also in counterhegemonic political constructions.

This framework sheds light on a growing concern with "security" in a context of more and more socioeconomic exclusion. The mirror image of our own fear of falling to the social margins is the abject image of the one who has been pushed there, to say nothing of the fear of retaliation or revenge at the hand of that other for what, with supposed ingenuity, we do when we refuse what Silvia Bleichmar termed decency—a deep sense of shame for benefitting at the cost of the suffering of the other.

All of these tools can be used in psychoanalysis from a gender perspective, that is, in clinical work that struggles not for tolerance or non-discrimination before that which is not intelligible (Butler, 2004) but that refrains from placing it a priori in the category of the psychopathological.

There is, in my view, a great deal of affinity between Butler (2005) and Bleichmar regarding how meaning is built around lives that "deserve to be lived" and deaths that "deserve to be cried over". Perhaps that is because both looked to Giorgio Agamben's concept of the "bare life", which refers to the life of the unequal and the abject, life afforded only the minimal conditions of biological survival but no transcendence or political meaning.

While it might seem easier to detect how these mechanisms of exclusion act on sexual- and identity-diverse populations than on women in general, they were unapologetically deployed against women until the twentieth century, when women were granted a number of basic citizenship rights in the West. That said, they are still evident in the crudest forms of patriarchy like femicides, human trafficking, and the violation of sexual and reproductive rights. On symbolic level, the idea that women should not aspire to recognition because they do not deserve it lives on.

"Who do they think they are? Do they really think they can go on vacation, study, read, go to the movies, eat good food, and stay warm all winter long? That's not for everyone" would seem to sum up the logic of neoliberalism. All of those "privileges" are only for certain people, deserving people, argues a limited conception of the peer.[14] What Agamben called bios is the life lived by those who merit that greater life, that is, for those who set standards regarding tastes, identities, and recognition. Zoe, or bare life, is for the excluded—and only for now, since they are left to die in a necropolitical regime.[15]

And here, true to Silvia Bleichmar's teaching, we must clarify that a psychoanalysis performed by and for citizens does not pursue wholesale absolution or liberation from guilt for those analysands who have acted unethically. When that is the case, clinicians participate in the production or consolidation of cynics. In feminist psychoanalysis, ethics and accountability are always part of clinical practice.

On the feminine, psychoanalysis's debts with men, and the revision of psychoanalysis's "gender theory" in Bleichmar's theoretic production and clinical work

Bleichmar's thinking on the relationship between subjectivity, the psyche, and power constitutes a major contribution for those of us working at the juncture between psychoanalysis and gender. And very different things can be said about the same topic. For instance, a structuralist position would hold that everything we need is in the founding texts in the field of psychoanalysis—all we have to do is find the right quote.[16] Others—among them me, in this chapter in particular—look to our mentors as a starting point for further work. At stake is breaking bonds that seem almost religious at times—in this case the "religion of the father" (Tort, 2005)—and going beyond exegesis.

My contact with Bleichmar's thinking was fundamental to my own theoretical work and a watershed in my clinical practice. When I met her, I was struggling with how to bring a gender perspective to bear on a binary and heteronormative psychoanalysis that explained away inequality as an intrapsychic or structural phenomenon. Inequality, the thinking went, was tied to the impact of sexual difference and the language generated by a single symbolic order, the only symbolic order possible.

I will now discuss how some of Bleichmar's contributions provide the groundwork for those of us who participate in the dialogue between psychoanalysis and gender.

The Feminine and Motherhood

Silvia Bleichmar theorises a political dimension to motherhood and reformulates the feminine in psychoanalytic production and theoretical work.

In the dedication to her book *No me hubiera gustado morirme en los 90*, for instance, she speaks of her mother as a political subject. She recounts an anecdote involving her brother, himself a psychoanalyst. He was worried about how their mother would be affected by the fact that her second husband was afflicted with a disease not unlike the one that had killed her first husband—the father of the both of them. Silvia countered her brother's concern with their mother in the sphere of the affective with a glib statement: "Mom can bury three husbands, but I doubt she will ever be able to part with socialism". With that, she positions her mother—and, I would venture to say, herself as well—as a subject deeply committed to social justice and redistribution. She envisions the political as no less central to the lives of women than the affective, no less dramatic in its impact on their vitality and spirit—and that is still an avant-garde assertion.

Bleichmar also rejected the Freudian formulation that sees a woman's desire to have a child as a means to make up for a lack (penis = child). She understood the desire to become a mother as bound to the desire for transcendence—a desire many psychoanalysts even today reserve for fatherhood. Bleichmar's thinking neither uproots women from the body nor reduces them to the body.

I am not sure if it is written anywhere, but I remember Silvia saying that what pregnancy and childbirth give women is, among other things, the experience of having confronted—and survived—the anguish of death. Motherhood placed in the realm of transcendence via cross-generational narcissism is a way not to die in a flood of self-love and not to need to appropriate the life of the other, which can only be enjoyed in mediated fashion. What could be further from the widespread idea of the maternal ravage?

On Sexual Diversity

Bleichmar used the phrase "to shuffle along" to describe how slow psychoanalysts in Argentina were to accepting the desire of same-sex couples to have children. While the opposition in Argentina did not go as far as it did in France where psychoanalysts openly disputed the PACs,[17] many were for a long time against at least the concept of diverse parenthood sanctioned by marriage equality. They argue that same-sex parents undermine the "right" of a child to have a "normal" family and, with it, what constitutes a "healthy" psyche.

Speeding things up rather than "shuffling along" as part of psychoanalysis's political project of casting off the ballast without disregard for the child means not allowing the explosion of the traditional association of procreation with coitus to cancel out what psychoanalysis discovered and what, among other things, it continues to work on, namely:

- The erotic nature of the tie between children and adults
- The role of sexuality in the constitution of the subject
- The regulation of sexual circulation required to enable the functioning of the psyche

The gender, object choice, and the sexed position of the adult primary caretaker is irrelevant to all of that.

Trans Childhoods

Bleichmar's book on masculinities (2006) makes some initial contributions to grappling with the issue of trans childhoods. She differentiates between a primary "surface transvestitism", something like a membrane or second skin around the self, on the one hand; and a diverse and consummated gender identity, on the other, a stable identity that must be considered. Gender identity is thus understood as acquired, as a trait formed in a primary identification process—an understanding in keeping with Dio Bleichmar's pioneering work on gender and identity (1985). Bleichmar's work along these lines has provided the groundwork for how contemporary psychoanalysts like myself and Facundo Blestcher envision trans childhoods (Meler, 2017).

Masculinities in Psychoanalysis

Bleichmar also made a fundamental contribution to the theory of masculinity in psychoanalysis (2006). Indeed, only recently has masculinity been addressed as a topic in psychoanalysis. In Freud, there is a theory of subjectivity and only that which differs from the masculine image in the mirror deserves study in specific texts like *Female Sexuality* (1964–1931) and *Femininity* (1964–1933). Bleichmar held that psychoanalysis had an ethical and clinical debt with men for having interpreted their fantasies of masculinisation—often expressed in the search for virility in a sexual relationship with another man—as homosexual fantasies. That facile equation cut short exploration of masculine anguish—and there in lies that debt.

Another contribution fundamental to those of us who work at the juncture between psychoanalysis and gender is Bleichmar's re-examination of the diagnosis of perversion. In her thinking, perversion is not determined by the sexual practice itself, a vision that has traditionally equated sexual diversity and perversion, but by the status of the other in the sexual encounter. Is that other a fellow subject or a mere object for the psyche? In other words, perversion lies in the objectification of the other—and that can happen in any sexual relation, including classic heterosexual pairings.

I am honoured to look to Bleichmar's rich body of work as a starting point, not as the last word—indeed, that is, arguably, the commitment we make to the psychoanalytic tradition. Many of us not only pay tribute to her as witnesses, but also carry on her legacy.

Notes

1 A first version of this text was delivered at the Panel Psicoanálisis, memoria y construcción política held in the context of the I Colloquium "Poniendo a trabajar Silvia Bleichmar", which took place Buenos Aires on August 5, 2017. I would like to thank Marina Calvo for the invitation to participate in an event that brought together her mother's countless disciples. The first written version of this piece was published in February 2019 in *RevistaTopia*.

2 An intellectual and free thinker, she was born in Bahía Blanca, Buenos Aires province on September 13, 1944, and died in Buenos Aires on August 15, 2007. She held a doctorate in psychoanalysis and master's degrees in psychology and sociology. She left Argentina in 1976, after the military coup staged that year, and settled in Mexico, where she remained until 1986. She received her doctorate from the Sorbonne, where her adviser was Jean Laplanche. She defended her dissertation in 1983. She returned to Argentina in 1986, now under democracy. She taught in graduate and master's degree programs at prestigious universities in Argentina, Mexico, Brazil, France, and Spain. The weekly seminars she gave for over ten years were attended by as many as 300 people and eventually published by Editorial Paidós thanks to the efforts of her disciples.

3 Freud and many of his followers, for instance.

4 Concept that we have previously introduced in the chapter dedicated to trans childhoods.

5 The idea that all subjects are equal from the get go, regardless of factors such as class, race, gender, geopolitics, sexual orientation, historical moment, cultural background, generation, and so forth.

6 After a devastating economic and political crisis, Argentina entered a post-Keynesian cycle in 2003. It lasted until 2015.

7 Translator's note: though unpublished in English, the title could be translated as "I Wouldn't Want to Have Died in the Nineties".

8 Very useful notions for working with victims of gender violence.

9 See Chapter 5.

10 In Spanish semejante.

11 See Chapter 5.

12 Some houses where victims of gender violence live also work with this logic.

13 That is, a critique of one very willing to help out, one who puts stock in "goodwill", but never looks into the material and symbolic conditions that make goodwill or its opposite, malevolence, possible.

14 These are questions that Bleichmar has asked herself in her texts.

15 On the basis of Foucault's notion of biopower as the sphere of life subject to power, the concepts of necropower and necropolitics describe the mechanisms that determine who can live and who must die. All modern states classify the lives of their subjects in a system where the death of certain bodies is not only expectable, but profitable. (Mbembe, 2019).

16 This topic is discussed at greater length in Chapter 9.

17 Analogous to civil unions in Argentina, *pactes civil de solidarité*, or Pacs, are available to partnerships where the two people are the same or not the same sex. Unlike marriage, Pacs to not confer kinship or eligibility to adopt children.

References

Agamben, G. (2003) *Stato di eccezione*, Bollati Boringhieri

Bleichmar, S. (2005) *La subjetividad en riesgo*, Editorial Topía

Bleichmar, S. (2006) *Paradojas de la sexualidad masculina*, Editorial Paidós

Butler, J. (2004) *Precarious Life: The Powers of Mourning and Violence*, Verso

Butler, J. (2005) *Giving an account of Oneself*, Fordham University Press

Dio Bleichmar, E. (1985) *El feminismo espontáneo de la histeria. Estudio de los trastornos narcisistas de la femineidad*, Siglo XXI

Freud, S. (1964) Female Sexuality, In *The Standard Edition of the Complete Psychological Works of Sigmund Freud, Volume XXI*. (1931) The Hogarth Press

Freud, S. (1964) New Introductory Lectures on Psychoanalysis, In *The Standard Edition of the Complete Psychological works of Sigmund Freud, Volume XXI*. (1933 [1932]) The Hogarth Press

García Reinoso, G. (1998) Reconocimiento del otro y de la articulación con el otro, para amar en el amor y en la amistad, en *Revista Postdata*, N° 2, Rosario

Mbembe, A. (2019) *Necropolitis*, Duke University Press

Meler, I. (2017) *Psicoanalisis y género Escritos sobre el amor, el trabajo, la sexualidad y la violencia*, Editorial Paidós

Tajer, D. (2009) *Heridos corazones. Vulnerabilidad coronaria en varones y mujeres*, Editorial Paidós

Tort, M. (2005) *Fin du dogme paternel*, Flammarion, Aubier

Chapter 8

Power Relations in Clinical Practice[1]

This chapter will discuss the little-recognised contributions Gilou García Reinoso[2] made to the theory and clinical practice of psychoanalysis from a gender perspective in Argentina, chief among them, in my view, her theorisation of the subject's relationship to power. Though she did not publish much—the bulk of her work was in clinical practice. She was also an activist,[3] often in institutional settings.

In one text (García Reinoso, 1997), she formulated the need for adults to *disidentify* with elements incorporated during early identification processes, specifically with elements related to generational asymmetry. To that asymmetry, I would add the asymmetries the patriarchal order produces in subjectivation. Patriarchy ensures that asymmetry, not necessarily between generations, lives on within a subject in later life stages. In other words, patriarchy reinforces intra-psychic asymmetry even when that asymmetry may not be operative on the level of the real in adult life.

She argues that processes of disidentification are as important as processes of identification, and that they have the potential to lead to freedom, conceived as recognition of, as opposed to disregard for, the other. According to her notion of freedom, otherness is not a synonym for one's relationship to that all-powerful parent (or first caregiver), overblown in size and scale for the child. She upheld the need to go beyond an interpretation that sees that other as an absolute narcissist, a vision that originates in childhood love, to make room for another figure in the adult psyche, the other envisioned as a peer in love and in friendship.

That line of work proves extremely useful for psychoanalysis from a gender perspective insofar as one of our primary tasks is to work through how the psyche internalises social power asymmetries passed on in childrearing. Through her theoretical model, we can observe that even in contexts where subjects have achieved at least the potential for greater equality, the remains of the introjection that takes place in early identification live on. At stake in that introjection is, among other things, gender contents and therefore power asymmetries. Introjection ends up binding subjects to the early incorporation of unequal difference in which gender and generation act together on personal relationships.

DOI: 10.4324/9781003411253-8

That asymmetry means, for instance, that in later stages of life women grant men a hegemonic position that certain men do not necessarily inhabit in their own lives as subjects. In other words, men are read by women as bearers of historical hegemonic prerogatives.

The image of "beheading the headless king" (Rosenberg, 1996) is poignant here. It captures the dynamics of women who at once submit to and confront any man, even if he does not position himself as dominant, because of the patriarchy women have internalised through primary processes of incorporating unequal difference. Gilou advocated the need to re-examine that identification in clinical practice. Indeed, she called for *disidentification* with the primordial other in relation to whom that asymmetry has been introjected. Such disidentification, she argued, would make it possible to relate to the other as a peer.

That formulation is valid for both genders, though the point of departure for each differs. For women, it is as the lesser, devalorised gender, whereas for men it is as the greater, hegemonic gender. The knot to untie is dense, and the path to equal relations long.

It is important to bear in mind that there are many ways to inhabit a gender. Stereotypes fail to capture the range of positions that a subject might adopt. No less important is the imposture subjects perform, imposing stereotypical traits and attitudes on themselves in order to be read as belonging to one gender or another.

Rereading Marie Langer[4] (1987), cofounder of the Asociacion Psicoanalitica Argentina (APA) and co-participant with García Reinoso, in the Grupo Plataforma's break from the APA in 1971,[5] we discover that she was also concerned with the roots of power relations in the psyche. Regarding Freud's "Totem and Taboo", Langer discusses how that totemic father was murdered to make it possible to "overcome the jealousy between brothers [...] Taken to a societal level, that means prioritising solidarity between peers over the wellbeing of the individual or the family or respect for the existing authority". That is in keeping with García Reinoso. The myth of killing the father acts as a metaphor for the importance of the intra-psychic work required for release from paternal authority figures for the sake of fraternal bonds of cooperation. As formulated by Freud and still taught today in orthodox psychoanalytic circles, that myth precludes the possibility of a female subject. Indeed, women are relegated to goods to be divvied up between male subjects.

It might seem a bit naive today to read literally Marie Langer's recommendation that a woman patient of hers not treat her husband as if he were her father but as if he were her brother. In the text referenced above (Langer, 1987), she states, "I told the woman quite frankly not to equate, in symbolic terms, her husband with her father, but with her brother so that she might form an alliance with him and other peers to fight the system...." The recommendation ignores that fact that relationships between sisters and brothers are also informed by the hierarchies of patriarchy. Brothers stand in for fathers by patriarchal mandate, enjoying male privileges—something that we are now better able to understand.

If we go beyond a literal reading of Langer, we see that the crux of her recommendation is to strengthen the modern values expressed in *liberté, égalité,* and *fraternité,* the rallying cry of the French revolution. Those first two terms in particular (freedom and equality) were embraced by feminist activists and academics until not long ago. More recently, the third term, *fraternité* or brotherhood, has been reworked and activated as sisterhood. A relevant antecedent to the concept of sisterhood is *afidamento,*[6] a term developed by feminists at Libreria de la Donna in Milan in the 1990s. Work remains to be done to develop a notion of siblinghood between men and women that does not naively ignore how sibling relationships as model are informed by patriarchal power asymmetries. A feminist understanding of siblinghood would also incorporate the hybrid masculinities resulting from the empowerment of women in recent years.

I mention Langer because, like García Reinoso, she recognised the importance of the fraternal, meaning bonds between equals. Neither contemplated, however, the gender inequality commonplace in sibling relationships between genders—an understanding central, in my view, to psychoanalysis's tasks of laying the psychological groundwork for reciprocal relationships. They were interested in working through the psychological obstacles to intra-gender and inter-gender alliances resulting from hierarchies within collections.

An inversion of Langer's appeal would, undoubtedly, have been interesting. What if she had warned a man against treating his life partner or wife like a child or daughter and urged that she be treated like a sister. It is, as I argued in Chapter 5, only now, after so many years of feminist struggle, that that inverted call can be issued.

Reformulating Psychoanalytic Theory on the Basis of García Reinoso's Contributions

In Chapter 3, I bring García Reinoso's contributions to bear on the relationship between psychoanalysis and gender. Her thinking helps us shatter the illusion of symmetry as a point of departure rather than as a point of arrival in a psyche constituted in the framework of patriarchal relations. Psychoanalysis from a gender perspective does not deny the reality of inequality but enables subjects to develop the potential that their life offers them. That means casting off not only the "gender corset" but also the introjection of the hierarchies that patriarchy imposes from the very beginning of the constitution of a subject's psyche.

Transformations and Effects in Clinical Practice

Employing this framework for interpretation and intervention in clinical practice has wonderful effects. García Reinoso herself was an unrivalled

psychoanalyst—and I say that from personal experience: she was my analyst for 20 years, and I am truly indebted and grateful to her (I have spoken
to fellow patients of hers and they have similar feelings). Her contributions
have major impact on clinical work insofar as they enable the deconstruction
of the marks patriarchy leaves on the psyche. Indeed, that was García Reinoso's genius. Contact with her in whatever capacity—as friend, student, or
patient—marked a watershed in terms of emancipation, vital stance, responsibility for oneself, and relationships with others. García Reinoso was interested in clinical work largely because it presented an opportunity to better life
with—and always *with*—others and with peers, regardless of degree of inti-
macy. That said, García Reynoso never called herself a feminist or explicitly
embraced a gender perspective in her work. But she was of French descent,
indeed she had lived in France for years, and she carried the "French Revolution in her bones", which meant her subjective appropriation of the notion of
the citizen was intense on the level of action—it was more than slogan. I had
arguments with her because she continued to uphold the singular importance
of the notion of sexual difference in psychoanalysis and the idea that there are
only two psychosexual positions. At one point, I said to her, "Come on Gilou,
let up with that!" She admitted that that notion of difference might not apply
to everyone, but it did apply to heterosexuals. In other words, she granted that
those terms are not universal. Not all loves, she admitted, are based on a desire
resulting from sexual difference and not all psychic structures understand castration of the self and the other as an inevitable consequence of recognising
sexual difference as the organiser of all differences. Indeed, desire and the
psyche can be structured around any number of things.

There were theoretical differences regarding the feminine and the masculine between García Reinoso and those of us who practise psychoanalysis from
a gender perspective. But her clinical work was extremely forward-looking.
For a feminist psychoanalyst like me—and I can say the same for the fellow
patients I ran into in her waiting room, among them individuals widely recognised for their contributions to society and culture—she greatly furthered our
ability to lead our lives with others.

She was the only woman psychoanalyst at a roundtable I attended com-
memorating the Plataforma and Documento groups historical break with the
APA in the 1970s.[7] She explained that accepting women psychoanalysts as
women had always been an issue, even for the progressive psychoanalysts
spearheading the break with the APA and its psychoanalytic orthodoxy.

She paraphrased Freud's response when women psychoanalysts would
complain to him about his remark that women do not contribute to culture.
Freud would say something like "No, no, *you* make a contribution, other
women do not". He saw his female disciples as exceptional and "masculin-
ised" women rather than as common women, whom he valued not at all.

García Reinoso was deeply troubled by this. She would say that even progressive or avant-garde psychoanalytic circles failed to "tolerate"—that was

her word—that a woman be a woman, that a powerful or intellectual woman be seen as something other than "a man in a skirt". She spoke of a supposed masculinisation not in relation to how women see themselves, but how men see powerful or enterprising women and ow they see intellectually brilliant women. She was not afraid to point out that male psychoanalysts, whether friends, co-workers, or husbands, disdained the time a woman spends mothering, especially if she refuses to give up her intellectual and professional development for the sake of motherhood.

Marie Langer says something similar when she thanks her husband for having supported her when she was dedicated exclusively to motherhood. I imagine that both women's experiences as psychoanalysts and mothers, and their shared attempts to coordinate those commitments, explains the coincidence.[8]

García Reynoso pointed out the subjective costs of the unequal distribution of both practical and symbolic care tasks between men and women. She would say that women, just like men, need "a wife" to help them take care of the house and family as well as to see to a social life often crucial to furthering their partner's careers.

A personal anecdote from my time as her patient. When my daughter was born, she said that I would have to take care of my baby, to be available to her, but without neglecting self-care. "You have to do what they tell you to do on aeroplanes", she said. "If you are travelling with children, put on your own mask first and then put your child's mask on her face". Her vision was at odds with the Difunta Correa myth[9] of the courageous mother found breastfeeding a child that outlives her. To bear that conviction out, she came to visit me when my daughter was one month old. When she left, she said, "I'll see you next Tuesday at my office", thus cutting short my cloistered postpartum period. She invited me to construct the space for the psychological and affective support my newborn needed and also to continue to tend to my own psychological space as a "non-mother" (Alizade, 1991).

I share that personal anecdote about Gilou the analyst so that it might form part of a long-ignored genealogy of women analysts, a tradition of which I form part as well. Their clinical and theoretical interventions are geared to providing children with what they need from childrearing for their psychological development but not at the cost of excessive maternal malaise. Mother and child, not mother or child, let alone child at the cost of the mother—always (Tajer, 2019).

Sexual Difference: The Organiser of All Differences in Psychoanalysis?

On that question, García Reinoso agreed with classic psychoanalysis—especially Lacanian psychoanalysis: sexual difference organises all other differences. Those of us who subscribe to psychoanalysis from a gender perspective think differently. We object to the a priori consensus regarding a symbolic order under patriarchy and heteronormativity for which there are only two positions. Other modes of symbolic organisation are possible, we argue. In other words, sexual difference is one difference among many. It is, of course, important, but it is not the sole difference that organises all others. And, by extension, not all desire is organised around sexual difference. That does not mean that those other desires disregard sexual difference. It is just that they are not caused by it.

Note: From 4:00 to 5:30 PM on November 28, 2018, I had the honour of organising a tribute to Gilou García Reinoso at the Universidad de Buenos Aires School of Psychology. The following participated as panelists: Martha Rosenberg, Marisa Rodulfo, Juan Carlos Volnovich, Rubén Efron, and Ana María Fernández through a text written for the occasion. The event can be viewed on youtube https://youtu.be/F3oE6WNDxHg

Notes

1 A first version of this chapter was published as *Entrevista a Débora Tajer*, in Revista Barquitos Pintados. Experiencia Rosario, N° 2, August 2018.
2 Gilou García Reinoso was a brilliant psychoanalyst who exercised significant influence on the cultural world of her time. She was, in a sense, a mentor with no disciples, an author with no books, a leader with no school. And despite that—or perhaps because of it, and the attendant style that meant she never fell into the common places that assure prestige and success—she became a figure revered by a number of generations of psychoanalysts. She was born on January 12, 1926, to a French family living in Villa Ballester, a small town on the outskirts of Buenos Aires. When Gilou was six, the family moved to Nice. They returned to Argentina in 1937, fleeing the impending war. After earning her medical degree, she went into analysis first with Arminda Aberastury and then with Willy Baranger. Though she was a full teaching member of the Asociación Psicoanalítica Argentina, she left that organisation to form part of the Plataforma group (see footnote 5). She was a founding member of the Asociación de Psicoterapia Psicoanalítica de Grupo. In the 1970s, she worked at the Teaching and Research Center of the Coordinadora de Trabajadores de Salud Mental and in the Medical Psychology Department and the School of Occupational Medicine of the Universidad de Buenos Aires School of Medicine. As an exile in Mexico during the military dictatorship in Argentina (1976–1985), she formed part of the Universidad Nacional Autónoma de México (UNAM) Institute of Occupational Medicine. She was a full member of the Asociación Mexicana de Psicoterapia Grupal and an honorary member of the Círculo Psicoanalítico Mexicano. Back in Argentina, she was the vice president of Médecins du monde and a member of the steering committee of the Permanent Assembly on Human Rights an independent non-governmental organisation. She died on May 23, 2018, at the age of 92 (Words in her honour written on the occasion of her death by her colleague and friend Juan Carlos Volnovich).
3 Largely in the sphere of human rights and the mental-health effects of state terrorism during the military dictatorship (1976–1983).
4 Marie Langer was the only female founding member of the APA (established in 1942). Born in Austria, she was forced to leave her country with the rise of Nazism. She worked as a doctor in the Spanish Civil War (1936–1939). She was one of the first psychoanalysts in Argentina to deal with the woman question from a feminist perspective. She and Gilou were friends. In 1971, they both broke with the APA for political reasons, forming part of Grupo Plataforma.

5 A groundbreaking association of psychoanalysts in Argentina. Informed by the events in Paris in May 1968 and political unrest closer to home, the group insisted on articulating the social and the psychoanalytic.

6 A concept used to render political the solidarity between women forged on the basis of "gender consciousness" (Kaplan, 1990) as constructed through feminist practice.

7 I remember that two of the panelists were Eduardo "Tato" Pavlovsky and Hernán Kesselman. I do not remember whether the third was Juan Carlos Volnovich or Fernando Ulloa.

8 Marie had four children, and Gilou three.

9 The story goes that Deolinda Correa de Bustos, a young mother in Santiago de Estero province in northern Argentina, died of dehydration during Argentina's civil wars while her baby survived, thanks to her breast milk.

References

Alizade, A.M. (1991) *Voces de Femineidad*, Edición de la autora

García Reinoso, G. (1997) Las relaciones del sujeto al poder, en *Revista Posdata*, Homo Sapiens editores

Kaplan, T. (1990) Conciencia femenina y acción colectiva: el caso de Barcelona, en James, S., Amelang y Nash, Mary (comps.), *Historia y género: las mujeres en la Europa Moderna y Contemporánea*, Ediciones Aldons el Magnánim

Langer, M. (1987) La mujer: sus limitaciones y potencialidades, en *Cuestionamos*, Editorial Búsqueda, Buenos Aires

Rosenberg, M. (1996) Género y sujeto de la diferencia sexual. El fantasma del feminismo, en Burín, Mabel y Dio Bleichmar, Emilce (comps.), *Género, Psicoanálisis y Subjetividad*, Editorial Paidós

Tajer, D. (2019), Prólogo, en Reid, G. *Maternidades en tiempos de des(e)obediencias. Versiones de una clínica contemporánea*. Noveduc

Chapter 9

Psychoanalysis Alone Is Not Enough, But We Can't Do Without It...[1]

The spread of the "green wave", as the pro-choice movement in Argentina is known, has led to new conversations and interests. Fellow psychoanalysts who had not felt drawn to feminism or gender studies before have become curious.

I believe that much of their interest is due to patients or teenagers in their own families who fight for abortion rights. They have also detected the emergence of a widespread social phenomenon that questions so many assumptions about femininities, masculinities, gender identity, and trans and non-binary issues, among other things. Prior to the feminist awakening, there was a certain conceptual stability, or at least a sense of it, around these issues in the psychoanalytic field.

This new questioning is both necessary and promising. The problem lies, however, in determining the conceptual framework in which the debate will take place. And that is where, in my view, we come upon the epistemological paradox that gives this chapter its title: Psychoanalysis alone is not enough, but we can't do without it.

Much of the work of some of my colleagues who attempts recently to dialogue with feminism is characterised by the following fallacies:

- Mistaking a dialogue between feminism and psychoanalysts that is novel for them as novel per se, that is, ignoring the history of theoretical production at that juncture
- Arguing that that dialogue should look only to the future, without verifying whether there is relevant previous work
- Using only the categories of psychoanalysis in the conversation with feminism, and refusing to give equal status in the debate to concepts coming from the field of gender and queer studies.
- Engaging only non-Argentine feminist authors who work in the field of philosophy (largely Butler and Preciado) and treating gender and queer studies as if they were one and the same
- Engagement that is largely limited to adolescent feminisms and its expressions on the social networks

DOI: 10.4324/9781003411253-9

- Mistaking the act of bringing a political dimension to bear on subjectivity for engaging in "activism in the office"

Having identified those fallacies, I will examine the assumptions I see, assumptions that must be addressed as interest in feminism grows. I will focus on issues that today's strains of feminism bring to the attention of psychoanalysis and psychoanalytic practice.

In my reading of recent texts where psychoanalysis is either questioned by or questions feminism, I have detected a powerful tendency to cast off anything that might seem threatening in an operation of the sort performed by a purified pleasure ego, a mode of subjectivity to which none of us is immune. At play here is psychoanalysis taking a stance on feminism wholesale. It is, in my view, necessary from the outset that each writer identify from which strain of psychoanalysis they are speaking and with which strain of feminism they are dialoguing—that because, as I have said throughout this book, there is not a single version of psychoanalysis or of feminism.

And among those many psychoanalyses and feminisms, there is a feminism that grapples with both fields and their articulation in highly complex terms.

The Specificity and Generality of Patriarchy

The singularities of the subjectivities we work with in psychoanalysis were constituted under patriarchy, a specific socio-historical model characterised by unequal differentiation between men and women. That does not mean that the notion of patriarchy can explain all aspects of human action and desire. It is one of many dialoguing concepts that must be added to the psychoanalyst's conceptual toolbox. Psychoanalysis from a gender perspective does not label everything patriarchy, the way what I call lay feminism[2] might, and that makes sense. After all, it is not fair to hold everyday speech to the standards of conceptual debate—it will always fall short. It is necessary, though, for psychoanalysis to sharpen its tools and prick up its ears to avoid treating as immutable truth concepts from the discipline that bears the previously invisible markings of gender inequality. Otherwise, those historical truths will be reproduced and psychoanalysis unwittingly act as yet another tool of social discipline.

Affective Accountability

Lay feminisms demand "affective accountability",[3] that is, that subjects take responsibility for their actions in their sexual and love relationship. A fundamental clarification here is that sex and love are not played out solely in the conscious or voluntary realm—and psychoanalysis from a gender perspective is well aware of that. Subjects must take accountability for their unconscious or involuntary actions as well their deliberate ones. In other words, one must take responsibility for oneself, one's whole self. But even that is not the entire picture. Accountability must be taken for what has come before any given subject—and appropriating our shared past is the work of a lifetime. We must give an account of ourselves (Butler, 2005). Lacan said as much as well when he re-examined the case of Dora (Lacan, 1966). He asks Dora, "What do you have to do with the problems of which you complain"?

Chapter 5 explores how contemporary men's processes of singularisation in the context of patriarchy lead them to set up a double ethical standard: women are not seen as peers or equals—and, I would argue, that is not true solely at an unconscious level. At play, rather, are cultural forms and forms of subjectivation, that is, things subjects may not really know themselves but that are not unconscious either. I am speaking of pre-conscious elements, things the subject cannot bring to light because of the paradigms in which the psyche is structured.

The everyday workings of what might be called the disparity device is what contemporary young women are getting at when they demand "affective accountability" on the part of their male peers. What they call for is an ethical stance that does not dismiss their desire as lesser than that of their male counterparts. They refuse to play by the rules of normative domination-based heterosexuality. I call those rules "the gender corset". A corset is stifling and uncomfortable for the one who wears it but allegedly pleasing to the one who looks at its wearer.

Adolescent young women condemn the double standard that earlier generations accepted and that much psychoanalysis still naturalises as a "masculine position" without questioning how it came into being, whether or not it has existed over the course of history, and what possibilities there might be for different modes of constituting masculinities.

The "green girls", as the young women in Argentina who have come of age with awareness of gender parity are called, realise that they can and should ask their male peers for "affective accountability", for democratic treatment as equals. They have seen that the males they interact with in their lives treat other young men and women, when they are friends, as equals, but that changes when the relationship is sexual or romantic. The opinions, explanations, and speculations of third parties aside, young women witness and experience—and condemn—that inequality, and we must listen to them.

"Affective accountability" means not hurting the other whenever it can be avoided. Far from a utopian ideal that pain can be dodged when love ends or is unrequited, at stake in the demand for "affective accountability" is avoiding excess suffering (Bleichmar, 2005) due to mistreatment, inconsideration, or "ghosting" of those who, historically, have not been seen as deserving of explanations or ethical regard.

Returning briefly to the question of intentionality, it is entirely possible that someone may have shirked "affective accountability" without meaning to or realising it. Regarding this, the rules of the game have, fortunately, changed a great deal. Much behaviour considered sexist today was, until not long ago, tolerated and even upheld as a model of "normal" masculinity. The question is how a young man acts when he realises how he has been behaving. Does he say, "Whoops, I messed up", recognising his role in the situation? Does he see it as something external to himself, that is, fail to see his own role in producing the situation? Or, upon coming to understand what has happened, does he take on the challenge of fighting that double standard?[4]

More is demanded of men today because there is greater awareness of the impunity they have enjoyed—and their female counterparts have not enjoyed—in the field of love and sex. This is coupled with another historical novelty: an entire generation of empowered young women who are taking on prerogatives once reserved for men. This generation has realised that the model of emancipation they have adapted is, in many ways, based on the autonomous model of hegemonic masculinity in modernity. But longstanding inhibition of hostility must not be mistaken for kindness,[5] and as young women are freer, they also have the ability to express what they want and do not want regardless of the reaction of others.[6]

This demand for accountability does not presume we always know what we want or that our lovers or partners do. Lay feminisms may habour that illusion to some extent, but it does not resonate in psychoanalysis from a gender perspective, which understands that we human beings are complex, conflicted subjects with an unconscious. That does not mean, though, that we cannot act ethically. Indeed, that complexity, rather than a hollow reading of subjectivity, is the basis for the call to accountability.

I would like, once again, to differentiate between the adolescent feminist wave in Argentina and, first, feminism as a whole and, second, psychoanalysis from a gender perspective, which has over 40 years of experience in Argentina articulating how psyches are constituted in the framework of patriarchal relationships.

One example of lay feminism's demand for greater "affective accountability" in heterosexual relationships revolves around the common failure of men to make contact with women after having had an often intense sexual or romantic encounter. Women complain that men "don't take the trouble" to offer explanations or even reach out if they are not interested in pursuing the relationship. They feel they are treated as if they were disposable, only as an object to be used for the man in question. They believe they are entitled to ethical consideration whereby the man would say to himself, "I am going to call her to tell her I don't want to keep seeing each other so she is not left hanging". The failure to make contact acts as an implicit farewell on the part of the man. No price is paid. That sort of masculine impunity is just one of men's prerogatives under patriarchy, one instance of not taking accountability for their own actions towards women. At play is, once again, not considering women peers deserving of the equal rights and consideration.

This lack of accountability is still possible because of the gender-based asymmetry—as opposed to mere difference—in the sex-romance market (Illouz, 2012). Men know that their worth on that market is higher than women's, thanks to patriarchal dividends:[7] men are not as attached to romantic love as women because they have centuries of experience separating love from sex and because their reproductive lives are so much longer than women's—and that gives them a power in this sphere that has not abated even as their power in others has. And men are quite willing to use that power. Indeed, this asymmetrical power distribution continues to be passed down to younger generations. One of the tasks for psychoanalysis from a gender perspective in its work with men constituted according to the hegemonic model is to make them take responsibility for their actions in the realm of romantic love and sex—that is, to help them develop an ethics even in this realm so that women and other "unequal" subjects come to be seen and treated as equals.

Many of my fellow psychoanalysts use the term "masculine position" to describe this cluster of phenomena. The implication is that any shift away from that sort of behaviour or that position would undermine masculinity understood as a single and monolithic thing—and that would place male subjects in the realm of the catastrophic. Furthermore, those colleagues formulate this from the place of an also singular and monolithic psychoanalysis. And it is in relation to those formulations that I say that psychoanalysis alone is not enough.

I recently had a conversation with a young man with an acute ethical compass. He told me he had never realised the avoidable pain the behaviour described above causes women. He explained that he, and many of his male friends, would not get in touch with women after encounters or offer any explanation for their "disappearance" because they did not want to create expectations. They believed that the woman in question would not be able to accept that they were not interested in pursuing a relationship even though the men valued the encounters. When I asked him if he would act that way in a professional situation or a friendship, he said he would not. He had never realised he used a double standard for sexual and romantic relationship with women—evidence that it is important to engage with men so they can begin to perceive the markings of patriarchy of which they are not aware. To do otherwise is to continue to naturalise patriarchy in clinical practice. We must not look for psychological explanations for what is a social construct.

All of this is related to the fact that the heterosexuality we know is not only normative but also based in domination. Luckily, it is not the only heterosexuality possible, and there are already openings and cracks in it through which something new is beginning to emerge. But meanwhile, we are still subject to that heterosexuality. And once again I assert that psychoanalysis is not enough to understand these phenomena; we must look to and construct categories capable of explaining them and the novelties in them. We must articulate the relationship between psychoanalysis, with its enormous power to grasp reality, and new concepts that understand subjectivation in socio-historical contexts.

What Phallocentrism Does Not Let Us See

The phallocentrism that continues to reign in psychoanalysis naturalises the fact that in the heterosexual regimen of domination the culmination and ideal of sexuality is penetration. There is nothing psychoanalysis has to say, nothing it has to offer, since it accepts that the ultimate truth for men is getting *it* up (or not getting *it* up)—the phrase itself indicates that the organ lies beyond a man's control. A man who can "get it up" occupies the "crowning masculine position". For that reason, psychoanalysis has trouble identifying the historical markings of a desiring regimen of domination where each man must make sure he is in charge so that he can deliver that "ultimate truth". That favourable outcome, the only one acceptable, is more feasible if the man is the one in control of the erotic scene and not overly implicated with his partner on an erotic or emotional level. That is another reason for the masculine disappearance mentioned above. At play is not only a lack of ethical consideration, but also flight as a defence against any scene where the man is not in control or in response to a ghost of passivation. That is by no means inevitable, however. It is, rather, just further evidence that in the regimen of domination there are only two possible pairings: leader or follower, meaning master or slave (Benjamin, 1995). If a man does not dominate, he fears he will be dominated.

Clinical intervention in psychoanalysis from a gender perspective might point out that there is not only one "true" form of masculinity; there are, rather, multiple masculinities. The idea would be to help pivot men towards a deconstruction of the markings of patriarchy in their erotic lives—the same demand that young feminists are making and, indeed, that early generations of women have made, desperate to enact new scripts with multiple and shifting positions in the erotic scene. The dance would be like jazz or queer tango[8]: over the course of a single song, who leads and who follows may change multiple times.

Strategic Essentialism

Some ask whether there is actually such a thing as men and women. First, we must discern, I would say, whether we are talking about essences or existences. To say that one does not believe in the existence of men and women is dubious in a culture where being signified as one or the other implies unequal access to economic and symbolic capital and where, furthermore, so many perceive themselves as either female or male.

And it is even trickier to call oneself a feminist if, like some thinkers, one does not believe that women exist. Amazing though it seems, that is just what some do, mostly speaking from a perspective that holds, though does not state explicitly, that feminism is no longer necessary. That is not the same, in my view, as arguing that masculinities and femininities are not a priori truths or essences but social constructs. To paraphrase Simone de Beauvoir, one is not born a woman (or a man) but becomes one.

The concept of "strategic essentialism" developed by Gayatri Chakravorty Spivak, a renowned postcolonial feminist thinker whose work engages psychoanalysis, makes a crucial contribution to this debate by formulating the need to shelve scepticism of innate essences and define a speaking subject for the sake of cohesive action. For psychoanalysis, that means putting aside caveats about essences to enable the construction of meaning in clinical work. In other words, we say that there are men and women not because we believe them to exist in essentialist terms, but because without those categories we cannot operate in the contemporary clinical reality. And this happens simultaneously with the existence of non-binary people whose challenge is to build existences outside the binary and heteronorma.

The Illusion of the Unique Self

There is, in my mind, a major and largely unaddressed contradiction in statements I have heard my fellow psychoanalysts make endless times. They claim not to believe in generalisations even though they have for years treated hysteria and obsessive neurosis as something like synonyms for femininity and masculinity, respectively. It is fundamental to distinguish between clinical work on specific cases and epidemiology—the distribution in a population of a given health problem, malaise, or psychological affliction. The tension between clinical work with individuals and epidemiology of course exceeds psychoanalysis; it is a factor in the broader relationship between clinical devices and populations (Almeida Filho, 2000). The basic tension resides in the fact that clinical work with individuals deals with modes of singularisation and the expression in daily life of wider currents, specifically ways of constructing subjectivity and what might be called cultural afflictions at a given historical juncture. Epidemiology, meanwhile, describes broader phenomena in social collectives, one of which is gender as category of belonging and identity. At play in the tension between sociology and psychoanalysis biases, then, is work with a specific someone who bears the markings of a historical moment and who experiences things that are similar to the things experienced by fellow members of the social collective they come from and identify with. *Similar* things, not the same things. Or, conversely, experiences that are singular—to a certain extent.

Psychoanalysts and/or Citizens

Great confusion sets in when categories designed for clinical work are applied to social phenomena. While psychoanalysis can *help* explain social phenomena—Freud himself attempted to do as much, with mixed success—it cannot in and of itself explain things that must be addressed from a broad perspective that looks to other branches of the social sciences (economics, sociology, anthropology, and gender studies, and others).

Similarly, the way those of us who practise psychoanalysis deal with our fellow citizens in the social sphere is different from how we deal with our patients—and the role of empathy is central to that difference. While empathy may well be an important aspect of a psychoanalyst's engagement in an institutional or political setting, or in their everyday dealings with others, it is not a primary tool for clinical practice. And I underscore not a *primary tool*—I do believe that a degree of empathy for the human pain experienced by the patient is essential to the clinical device.[9] A *degree* of empathy—a careful balance must be struck to enable the hospitality of the clinical device (Ulloa, 1996) without assuming or assigning a priori meaning to what patients tell us, one of the risks that comes with empathy. I by no means disavow empathy, just believe it is important to be aware of the risks it poses. Once again, that applies only to clinical work. In daily life, the lack of empathy can lead to cynicism. Empathy is crucial to attempts to analyse social phenomena from a psychoanalytic perspective.

The Psychological Effects of *The Beauty and the Beast* on Feminine Sentimental Education

Psychoanalysis alone is not enough, but without it we cannot grasp how a woman might think that a man who treated another woman poorly would act differently with her. Or when on a first date she senses "something is off" but sees him again because she mistrusts her own perception ("you never think anyone is ever good enough for you"). Psychoanalysis alone is not enough because we must take into account the enormous impact of the romantic ideal and ideals of traditional femininity fomented in the culture and reinforced time and again in the rearing and sentimental education of girls by stories like *The Beauty and the* Beast (Illouz, 2012). At the same time, without psychoanalysis it is not possible to pinpoint how those social ideals are internalised or operate in the psyche. They might act as the contents of the ego ideal or the superego, or they might act as a defence mechanism against forms of suffering. A model that addresses the relationship between the psychoanalytic and the social, each with its particular intellectual tradition, must be developed, a model that loses neither the specificity nor the efficacy of either field.

Furthermore, patriarchy is neither a category that can explain everything nor one external to our individual subjectivities. We construct ourselves as subjects under patriarchy, and its markings are found throughout our subjectivities and subjectivation, here regarding a romantic ideal that erotises the tie to the social master, that is, the man-beast.

Deconstruction

Useful here is Derrida's notion of deconstruction (1989) imported, so to speak, from the fields of philosophy and literary criticism to the analysis of subjectivities. More than men, modes of desire are what must be deconstructed, along with the expectations and ideals enmeshed in inequality and imparity, particularly in the field of language, the sphere where each subject articulates their discourse and account of themselves. The process of deconstruction attempts to open up other possible approaches to the complex ways desire and power are bound.

Once again, and at the risk of being heavy-handed, it is not a question of discerning where patriarchy ends and the self begins. I am myself, him, her, them, us, they, and so forth *in* patriarchy.

That said, there are different ways of being and being in patriarchy.[10] Again, these are types useful to the task of classifying and understanding, but in practice they appear within us, our relationships, and our social world in all sorts of combinations, generating countless tensions and conflicts.

At the same time, the specific ways desire and power are articulated vary between those who have undergone subjectivation to form part of the hegemonic gender and those who have undergone subjectivation to form part of the subjugated gender. And that, in turn, is connected in different ways to how power is (or is not) accumulated and to how inequality is experienced in the social world according to categories (ethnicity, class, age, sexual orientation, physical ability, nationality, caste, etc.). "Intersectionality" is the term for those multiple layers of inequality. Coined in the 1990s by Black feminist activists in the third feminist wave in the United States,[11] it describes how gender, race, and class work together in forms of social and subjective inequality.

Toxic Subjectivities or the Poison of Inequality?

In keeping with the second part of the title of this chapter ("we can't do without psychoanalysis"), I agree with those who point out the vagueness and deficiency of the notion of "toxic individuals" or "toxic relationships" so widespread among young (and not so young) feminists. I understand that it might be useful in everyday life to identifying relationships and people who do not contribute to our well-being (it is, after all, an example of lay feminist "plebian wisdom").[12] The notion of toxicity is not, however, useful to those of us who work in psychoanalysis from a gender perspective. That said, it does lay bare the inequality and inequity in the relationships it describes. In these relationships, one person is affected and the other capable of inflicting harm, one takes more than they give and takes advantage of the other. Hidden in the narrative of the 'toxic relationship' is, in my view, a lack of explanation of how and why the one who is stuck stayed and the reasons why he or she keeps taking the 'poison'. That question by no means implies that the two parties are equally responsible (they are not because they are not equal). Taking a look at what is actually happening does not necessarily mean accepting responsibility or blame—and that is important to bear in mind.

In my view, the notion of "toxicity" applied to relationships has no place in clinical practice. Its blunt vision reduces the complexity of what it attempts to examine. It suggests that a relationship's problems can be resolved by taking distance from or not seeing the "toxic" person. That means we lose the opportunity to grapple with the attraction to what is toxic, as well as a whole set of ambivalences and contradictions—and since very early on, psychoanalysis has taught us that we do not always pursue what does us good. I urge lay feminisms to pay attention to the fact that the simplification of complexity can be detrimental to their ability to achieve greater emancipation.

Psychopathy or Impunity in the Exercise of Power?

The use of the term "psychopath" in daily life is not unlike the use of "toxic". A person who wields power in a relationship or objectifies their partner is not necessarily perverse, even if those actions and attitudes are. What is really at stake is not the psychic inability to recognise the existence of an other as a subject, but the deployment of double standards: some deserve consideration and others do not..[13] In its most extreme forms, that double standard can take the shape of *chineo*—something common and widely tolerated in traditional regions of Argentina with high levels of social inequality. *Chineo* refers to a practice whereby wealthy young men have their way with young women from poorer social sectors. More specifically, the men feel entitled to those women's bodies; they believe they can do whatever they want sexually with or without those women's consent—an attitude they would never assume with women from the same social sector. In fact, there might be a sort of "implicit" consent to certain actions, even though they put the woman at risk, because she hopes to "get with" a guy in a better position.[14] On many occasions, things end terribly.[15]

From the "Love Police"[16] to Innovative Self-Esteem

I share the concerns of some of my fellow psychoanalysts regarding what we might call the love police. I understand that one of the most important achievements in recent years is the right to publicly love and desire whomever it is we love and desire, and for those relationships to be accepted as legitimate. It is now possible to exist out in the open as LGTTBI+, and perhaps one day hetero will be just another possible sexual choice, not the norm. One can be monogamous, polygamous, polyamorous, or celibate by choice. There is no longer a "normal sexuality"—and the attempts of any strain of feminism to impose one must be disregarded and combated. The feminist movement, as a movement for liberation, must not become a new master.

I would like now to return to some ideas I developed years ago regarding what I called the ideal affliction (Tajer, 2009), that is, subjection to ideals, even ideals of freedom and liberation. And combating that affliction is unquestionably something psychoanalysis has to contribute to feminism. But it can only do that if it re-examines its own heteronormativity, the markings of binary patriarchal and colonial thinking that it too bears—its own ideal affliction.

Similarly, before levelling criticism at "lay feminisms" for the emphasis they place on self-love, it is necessary to analyse gender differences in the construction of self-esteem as one of the components of narcissism discussed in Chapter 1. Female narcissism according to traditional femininity is based on "being for others"; what is under construction now is an alternative and innovative narcissism grounded on "being for oneself"—a historical novelty. In clinical work with individual patients, it is our task as feminist psychoanalysts to accompany contemporary women in the often complex passage from the old model of narcissistic construction to the new one.

Public Shaming and "Cancelling": Grassroots Actions against Abuse and Impunity

Something else that troubles many of my fellow psychoanalysts is public shaming in high schools.[17] I mention it here because it has been at the heart of recent questioning of feminism from the psychoanalytic field. The feeling seems to be that feminism has "gotten out of hand".

Public shaming has come to the attention of many psychoanalysts through cases in their clinical practice, their families, or their circle of friends. Many of the high schools where shaming practices[18] have become controversial are attended by children of psychoanalysts or their patients, likely because those schools largely service a social sector for which psychoanalysis is one of the devices available when issues like this come up. For that reason, I believe we must be prepared (see Chapter 2) to deal with these situations. That means, first off, recognising that many of this burning gender issues today are played out among adolescent students from culturally privileged sectors. Once again here, psychoanalysis alone is not enough, but we cannot do without it.

In articles on psychology, I have read in the newspaper or pop psychology magazines, and in my own interventions at schools, I have noticed a reduction of feminism to public-shaming practices deemed reprehensible. It is as if a still from a complex film were mistaken for the entire movie. What is omitted is that these shaming practices emerged from the bottom up as a means of self-defence against situations at school—where young men had been repeatedly abusive towards young women or their non-sexually or identity conforming peers. Public shaming was a response to the inability or unwillingness of school authorities or families to deal with—that is, prevent or stop—ongoing abuse. They were, then, a means to democratise distress in times when acts of harassment and abuse largely went ignored or unpunished. But all of that has been left out of the reading. Instead, emphasis has been placed on the negative impact on the lives of the "shamed" young men without taking in the whole picture, which includes historical suffering on the part of women young and old due to harassment and abuse. That simplistic reduction does not capture the complex dynamic or, therefore, the logic of shaming. The observation of one female student is on target: "The schools only called you when things got rough for the male students". That student speaks a powerful truth about institutions and the society that houses and creates them: the alarms do not go off until the ones who really matter are affected (Butler, 2004).

Unfortunately, it is often still true today, albeit involuntarily, that the suffering of men is seen as more important than the suffering of women in clinical practice. Furthermore, the suffering of some men—the ones that form part of hegemonic groups—is taken more seriously than the suffering of other men—the ones that for an array of reasons (ethnicity, race, class, sexual orientation, etc.) are considered lesser.[19] It concerns me, then, that fellow psychoanalysts are so very worried about the suffering of young men in public shaming; it shows the enduring marks of patriarchy on psychoanalysis and harks back to the discipline's origins when cases of girls sexual abuse at the hands of fathers were invisibilised by the theory of seduction[20] (Volnovich, 2017).

My position on public shaming and its larger context embraces prevention, not punishment. I believe in the need to work towards a cultural change that places emphasis on childhood and adolescence as constituent moments in subjectivation. We must start at those early phases; otherwise, we will be too late.

It is pointless, in my view, to punish young men for abusive sexist behaviour without acknowledging that they are simply doing what they have been taught to do and that they are acting according to models for the ideals of hegemonic masculinity. These teenage boys are neither bad nor sick, but rather *healthy sons of patriarchy.*[21] And that sad fact implies a social responsibility that goes beyond schools, which are just a sound box of what is happening in the broader historical-social context. On that basis, it is important to identify what type of clinical intervention is most suited to which act of sexual aggression without ignoring the overriding logic that binds them all together. No less important is developing broader clinical models in what Fernando Ulloa calls "social numerosities" (Ulloa, 2004), that is, clinical tools to grapple collectively with a problem that has singular but also general aspects.

That awareness of a broader clinical practice with varying levels of intervention informed how I handled the accusations of abuse and public shaming or cancellation at a high school in Buenos Aires when, in early 2018, a group of psychoanalysts who were also mothers at the school went to the school administration about the problem.

In that framework, activities were organised throughout the school year. The programme revolved around nine workshops that included students, teachers, and families. The idea was to open up a non-punitive channel for group processing of the problems facing gender relations at the institution. That approach allowed us, to return to the metaphor above, to see the whole film, not just the public shaming which, as mentioned, was what set off the alarms at the school and in the families (Tajer et al., 2020).

That broader vision sheds light on a true and historic change in adolescent gender relations that is expressed in many ways. Young women do not want to put on the "gender corset" described above; they reject the idea that women must be careful not to "provoke" "unbridled" masculine sexuality; they want parity and freedom; they want to feel safe. The young men taking their first steps into the terrain of romantic love and sex do so on the basis of the model of hegemonic masculinity, the model under which they became subjects, even though they do not necessarily share its ideals. That in no way means they are victims of patriarchy, but rather unwitting participants in or accomplices of it. The young men and women agree that the binary model of division into only two genders is outdated—a model that informs the assignment of bathrooms, school uniforms, and sports requirements, to name a few. The students uphold the need to visibilise trans and non-binary classmates.

Complicity here is not understood in the legal sense, but in terms of subjective accountability. It is the term Connell (1997), a specialist in masculinity studies, uses to describe how a great many men relate to the hegemonic project. What the term gets at are individuals with masculinities constructed such that they receive the patriarchal dividend without having to take on the risks that come with being on the "front lines" of patriarchy. Patriarchy's accomplices must be supported as they attempt to position themselves differently. More flexible models of masculinity must be articulated, models committed to self-care and care for others.

The work at the school also brought to light the "gender" of the institution itself. Many of the patriarchal attitudes of male students were tolerated, when not encouraged or supported, by the adults at the institution. Over the course of our work, former students spoke out about situations they had endured at the hand of teachers and administrators, which affirmed in no uncertain terms the need to undertake the arduous task of deconstructing the school's patriarchal practices and do away with institutional impunity. We must make sure acts of violence are not repeated going forward (Tajer, 2022).

The experience at the school was very meaningful. We were not, of course, able to work out all the problems, but we did help cool things off, abate cruelty, and ease distress. In fact, thanks to the positive attention the project received, the model is being repeated at other schools. The experience reaffirms the need for collective processing of cultural changes around gender, as well as, in some cases, individual clinical work.

Consent: A Contribution from the Imagination of Radical Youth

In the work with high schools, I experienced firsthand youth's creativity when it comes to solving problems. Despite widespread cultural stereotypes, youth is much more than a population to be monitored and punished. Young people's creativity is evident in how they understand consent, namely, asking explicitly if the other person in an encounter wants the same thing as the person asking the question does, and accepting the response whatever it may be. Rather than de-eroticise, the consent device enables young people to sustain desire and love without inflicting pain or engaging in abuse.[22] It occurs to me that consent today acts like condoms in the 1980s and 1990s at the height of the HIV/AIDS pandemic. Just as at that time the condom turned into an ally that made it possible to keep having sex, today consent makes it possible to navigate the current epidemic of cruelty unleashed by the fall of modernity's sexual order while another model is in formation.

Inheritance Work: Owning Tradition

Another complex issue I would like to address briefly as I bring this chapter to a close is the belief that the founding texts of psychoanalysis are capable of accounting for the current implosion of the modern sexual order and the resulting disarray in gender relations. If exacting exegesis were performed on every last word of those texts, this position seems to hold, they would be able to illuminate today's clinical challenges. That approach is not only futile, in my view, but also misguided. Its premise is not that those of us who bring other frameworks to bear on psychoanalysis have a different vision, but rather that we have failed to grasp psychoanalysis's "message".

Along these lines, I ask myself whether the notion of "misunderstanding between the sexes" (Miller, 2018) can encompass all the nuances of gender and sexual diversity. Once again, that might be a good starting point, but alone that formulation is not enough.

Nor is psychoanalysis alone enough to grapple with diverse identities or even with the current (mis)understandings and con/divergences in the "hetero world". Much of what has been written about romantic love and sex between cis and heterosexual women and men assumes that the male is the agent and the woman the seductress who puts off consummation. In that framework, a man ambivalent about consummation can (or, more accurately, could) make advances anyway because the woman will (again, would) frustrate them. But today seduction follows another script, and we will never bring the players closer together by "masculinising men" or "feminising women". That ship has sailed, and many will never turn back.

Nor can we say with any certainty today that the "feminine" is drawn to the "masculine" or vice versa. That myopic view does not allow us to see queer heterosexual ties where, for instance, a "feminised" heterosexual man wants to be with a "feminine" woman so they can be "girls together". Or when a "masculine" heterosexual woman wants a man who can be both "masculine" and "feminine" with her (Dío Bleichmar, 2010, pp. 213–214).

Another key issue is the status psychoanalysis grants its interlocutor, in this case feminism. To envision it as just "a passing discourse that we have no choice but to dialogue with" (Miller, 2018) is not a valid starting point.

Feminism is not a passing trend. It is more than a discursive device or montage to organise the real. Feminism is a change in the real, and hence in its discourses, in how the real makes meaning. It is a profound shift in the power relations between genders. It is the end of a world, but not the end of the world. And that radical change leads to new needs and positions. Because feminism is so far-reaching, it requires a change in psychoanalysis if psychoanalysis hopes to stay relevant and not lose the avant-garde mission at its origin. And that dismissal of feminism, of its depth, poses a serious risk to psychoanalysis. Might it be acting as a shield? Might feminism be a false enemy to keep psychoanalysis together as it runs the risk of imploding due to its own inconsistencies? Psychoanalysis, in my view, is worthy of a nobler fate.

The concept and term "gender" is often criticised as foreign, as an import from English.[23] I disagree with that analysis of the term, but even if it were foreign, it is deserving of hospitality. There is nothing less psychoanalytic than indiscriminately rejecting other discourses, discourses that come from elsewhere.

Another line of thought equates science and capitalism and considers feminism part of that whole.[24] That facile thinking fails to see that *some* science is at the service of the market and objectification. A rights-based science, however, puts limits on the market and heeds the needs of the subject, among them the need to take time to work through ambivalence about dramatic interventions on their body. It is not the same as a science that seeks only sales. For that science, any new group—including feminists—is a target market. But psychoanalysis, itself a scientific discourse (among other things), should be able to unravel those discourses and differentiate truth and genuine speech from appropriation and market interests.

Lastly, I would like to challenge the ongoing notion that the psyche's sole engine is sexual desire and its search for satisfaction, a perspective that disregards the current research. The human psyche, that research has found, is organised in a number of systems that work in parallel. The interaction between those various systems and their motivations, on the one hand, and sexuality, on the other, is highly complex, and the degree of activation or predominance of one or another varies.

Finally, I beseech you to prevent a practice that was once avant-garde from becoming an ally of the most reactionary and conservative forces of these times, thus turning psychoanalysis into a shameful discipline. That means, among other things, looking to the work of the discipline's greats not as the last word but as a tradition to work through and with, to formulate a dialogue between that tradition and current modes of pleasure and pain.

Notes

1 A first version of this chapter was published on June 8, 2019, on the news portal Latfem (www.latfem.org) under the title "Descubrir la pólvora. Les feministes menos pensades".

2 I use this term to describe feminist practices that do not produce or attempt to produce specific knowledge but rather to resolve the problems of everyday political and social life. Whereas academic or intellectual feminism must be rigorous in the concepts it designs, lay feminism does not have that responsibility.

3 A term used by youth feminisms to make visible the importance of taking responsibility for the impact of love and sexual decisions. Taking into account the effect on others and not only on oneself.

4 I spoke of the relationship between impunity and hegemony in subjectivation in my Ted Talk on October 23 and 24, 2019, available at //youtu.be/bLk4NwOdeeQ. In the article "Porque el rugby" published as the full back-page article in *Página 12* newspaper on January 23, 2020, I apply the notions of impunity and hegemony to another situation https://www.pagina12.com.ar/243249-por-que-el-rugby.

5 I look here to Irene Meler's very lucid observation that women, like other subordinate groups, have internalised a social prohibition against openly express hostility. What might be mistaken for kindness is in fact inhibited hostility. At historical moments when women have the right to express their hostility, they are faced with the ethical challenge of how to do so. This mechanism is explained in greater depth in Chapter 1.

6 On this point, see Fernández (1993).

7 Patriarchal dividends refer to the social privileges men enjoy under patriarchy simply because they belong to the dominant gender group. Those dividends include more free time, greater sexual freedom, fewer domestic obligations, and a voice with greater authority, to name a few.

8 In queer tango, as opposed to classic tango, which dancer leads (the male in traditional tango) and which one follows (the female in traditional tango) may change over the course of the dance.

9 Sandor Ferenczi developed the notion of empathy as a powerful engine of the psychoanalytic cure. His contributions on this topic are summed up in a book with the suggestive title in Spanish "Sin simpatía no hay curación" (Ferenczi, 2008).

10 See Chapter 1.

11 The concept of intersectionality was coined in 1989 by Kimberlé Williams Crenshaw, a US-American academic and professor specialised in the field of critical race theory.

12 I take the term from Néstor Perlongher (Bellucci and Palmeiro, 2013). He used it to describe the wisdom constructed in everyday social practices and recognised that that wisdom is often deeper and more complex than academic ways of naming those same practices.

13 See Chapter 5.

14 At play in this romantic ideal is the figure of Cinderella.

15 They did for María Soledad Morales in Catamarca province. A young student soon to turn 18, she was murdered on September 8, 1990, by two "sons of power", unleashing a political crisis with national implications. She went to a party with young men of her age from the dominant social class, the sons of politically powerful families, unsuspecting that they would treat her, as a working-class dark-skinned woman, like an object. Drugged and sexually abused, she went missing for a number of days before appearing dead. A nun who taught at her school led a protest to bring to light the events. The case drew public attention around the country.

16 The term in Spanish is *policia afectiva*. It refers to the peer policing of doing what is supposed to be done. An example of this is that a feminist cannot be in love with or desire a patriarchal man, or cannot be monogamous if she wishes to be, among other things.

17 I was invited to numerous roundtables and other activities that discussed these issues in 2018 and 2019.

18 The term used in Spanish for Argentina is *escraches* and for Chile is *funas*. It is a practice invented by the human rights group HIJOS (children of the disappeared). Faced with impunity, they began to make visible who had been the appropriators and murderers of their fathers. This tradition was taken up in 2015 by youth feminisms in Argentina and later in Chile to make visible male abusers who were unpunished. By means of posters or posts on social networks. See in the book that I compiled under the name of Psicologia Feminista (Tajer, 2022) the debate on that topic and the work of our team in middle schools in Buenos Aires.

19 In the article "Porque el rugby?" mentioned in footnote no. 4, I discuss how imaginaries of masculinity, class, and race conspired in the scene that ended in the murder of 18-year-old Fernando Baez Sosa in the beach town of Villa Gesell in the austral summer of 2020. The dark-skinned son of a working-class family, Baez Sosa was killed by a group of young men who acted with total impunity and lack of empathy for one whom they did not consider a peer.

20 Freud eventually changed his position, eschewing the idea of seduction and recognising hysteria as a response to real experiences of sexual abuse. He later discovered the fundamental importance of fantasy to hysteria and understood neurosis as constituted on the basis of the fantasies of girls and female adolescents. By abandoning the theory of seduction, he furthered the invisibilisation of real cases of abuse. Psychoanalysis from a gender perspective examines how real abuse and the fantasies of the person abused are enmeshed—one *and* the other, not one *or* the other in a binary logic.

21 A concept coined by Eva Giberti, one of the pioneers in Argentina in the social dissemination of psychoanalysis in the media.

22 I once again reference my October 2019 Ted Talk which discusses the takeaways from this experience https://youtu.be/bLk4NwOdeeQ?si=uyxUSovaufWdWUUT.

23 In French and Spanish spoken psychoanalysis.

24 That is how a major strain of French Lacanism sees its (Miller, 2018).

References

Almeida Filho, N. (2000) *La ciencia tímida. Ensayos de deconstrucción de la epidemiología*, Lugar Editorial

Bellucci, M., & y Palmeiro, C. (2013) Lo queer en las pampas criollas, argentinas y vernáculas, en Fernandez A.M. y Siqueria Peres, W. (comps.), *La diferencia desquiciada. Géneros y diversidades sexuales*. Editorial Biblos

Benjamin. J. (1995) *Like subjets, like objets. Essays on recognition and sexual difference*. Yale University Press

Bleichmar, S. (2005) *La subjetividad en riesgo*, Editorial Topía

Butler, J. (2004) *Precarious Life: The Powers of Mourning and Violence*, Verso

Butler, J. (2005) *Giving an account of Oneself*, Fordham University Press

Connell, R.W. (1997) La organización Social de la Masculinidad, en Valdés, T. y Olavarría, J. (eds.), *Masculinidad/es. Poder y Crisis*, Ediciones de las Mujeres

Derrida, J. (1989) *La deconstrucción en las fronteras de la filosofía. La retirada de la metáfora*, Editorial Paidós

Dio Bleichmar, E. (2010) Cuestionario, en Beatriz, Zelcer (comp.) *Diversidad Sexual*, Lugar Editorial

Ferenczi, S. (2008) *Sin simpatía no hay curación. Diario clínico de 1932*. Editorial Amorrortu

Fernández, A.M. (1993) *La mujer de la ilusión. Pactos y contratos entre hombres y mujeres*. Paidós

Illouz, E. (2012) *Pourquoi l'amour fait mal, L'expérience amoureuse dans la modernité*, Seuil

Lacan, J. (1966) *écrits 2*, Seuil

Miller, J.A. (2018) Encuentro con Jacques Alain Miller, en *Feminismos Variaciones Controversias*, EOL, Grama

Tajer, D. (2009) *Heridos corazones. Vulnerabilidad coronaria en varones y mujeres*, Editorial Paidós

Tajer, D., De la Sovera, S. & Lavarello, M.L. (2020) Hijxs y nietxs del #NiUnaMenos. Dispositivo de trabajo con malestares entre los géneros en una escuela secundaria en tiempos de democratización de las incomodidades, en Tajer, Débora (comp.), *Niñez, adolescencia y género. Herramientas insterdisciplinarias para equipos de salud y educación*, Editorial Noveduc

Tajer, D. (2022) Denuncias de abuso y escraches: sin impunidad y sin punitivismo. Una salida colectiva, en Tajer, Débora (comp.), *Psicología Feminista*, Editorial Topía

Ulloa, F. (1996), *Novela clínica psicoanalítica. Historial de una práctica*, Editorial Paidós

Ulloa, F. (2004) Prólogo, en *Las Huellas de la Memoria. Psicoanálisis y Salud Mental en la Argentina de los 60' y 70'*, Tomo I: 1957–1969, Editorial Topía

Volnovich, J.C. (2017) Aquellos vientos trajeron esos lodos, en Meler, Irene (comp.), *Psicoanálisis y género. Escritos sobre el amor, el trabajo, la sexualidad y la violencia*, Editorial Paidós

Index

ability to control 12
abject 28, 62, 65, 79
account 15, 20, 48, 61, 76, 84, 94, 95, 99, 100, 107, 109
accountability 72, 76, 77, 80, 93–96, 104; lack of 72, 77; subjetive 76
accountable 61, 68, 76, 77; affectivelly 76
activism in the office 93
afidamento 87
Agamben 78–80, 84
Alizade 89, 91
Alkolombre 16, 29
Amorós 70, 73
Amorós Puente 70, 73
Amphibians 67, 69, 71, 73
Asociacion Psicoana-litica Argentina 86
asymmetry 6, 8, 9, 15, 33, 35, 85, 86, 96
autonomous model 95
Ayouch 43, 60, 66

Badinter 13, 16, 32, 43
Barzani 49, 57
Beauty and the Beast 99
Benjamin 16, 33, 43, 52, 57, 61, 66, 70, 73, 108
Berkins 48, 53, 57
binary 24, 30, 31, 35, 37, 41, 43, 47, 57, 80, 92, 98, 102, 104, 108; thinking 98
bios 77
Bleichmar 22, 24, 29, 32, 37, 39, 42–45, 49, 51, 55, 57, 62, 66, 74–84, 91, 94, 106, 109
Blestcher 42, 55, 57, 82
Bourdieu 12, 16, 60, 66
bourgeois science 19

Braidotti 35, 43
Butler 19, 28, 29, 36, 44, 53–55, 57, 65, 66, 79, 84, 92, 94, 103, 109

cancelling 102
Caro Hollander 43
Chakravorty Spivak 98
childrearing 3, 8, 20–28, 40, 57, 59, 85, 89
chonguear 14
cis person 50, 52
citizen 76, 88
citizenry 75
citizenship 76, 79
Clavero 57
Closet 58
complicity 104
Connell 29, 53, 104, 109
consent 105
constitution of the psyche 3, 23, 33, 37, 49–52, 74, 75

deconstruction 36, 88, 97, 100
Deleuze 35
democratise distress 103
Derrida 59, 100, 109
deserve to 79
desire 4, 6, 16, 21–27, 30–32, 34–37, 40, 43, 49, 52, 53, 59–61, 65, 67, 69, 71, 73, 81, 88, 90, 93, 94, 100, 101, 105, 106, 108; of the child 100
desiring 21, 22, 46, 49, 52, 53, 75, 97
desiring spiritualism 49, 75
devalued gender 21
device 19, 21, 28, 47, 55, 62, 76, 94, 99, 105, 106; biopolitical 55
dictatorship 27, 29, 43, 47, 76, 90

For Product Safety Concerns and Information please contact our EU
representative GPSR@taylorandfrancis.com
Taylor & Francis Verlag GmbH, Kaufingerstraße 24, 80331 München, Germany